Game Changers: The Greatest Sports Stories .

Copyright © 2024 J.Berryman

All rights reserved. No part of this book may be reproduced, distributed, or transmitted in any form or by any means, including photocopying, recording, or other electronic or mechanical methods, without the prior written permission of the publisher, except in the case of brief quotations embodied in critical reviews and certain other noncommercial uses permitted by copyright law. For permission requests, write to the publisher at the address below.

publishing@jberryman.co.uk

Disclaimer: The information contained in this book is for general informational purposes only. While the author has endeavoured to provide accurate and up-to-date information, the author makes no representations or warranties of any kind, express or implied, about the completeness, accuracy, reliability, suitability, or availability with respect to the information, products, services, or related graphics contained in the book for any purpose. Any reliance you place on such information is therefore strictly at your own risk.

Game Changers: The Greatest Sports Stories Ever Told

Forward

Welcome to a treasure trove of sporting legends, the kind of epic tales that you've probably heard a thousand times at family gatherings, barbecues, and every pub in town. These are the stories that make people's eyes light up, the ones they recount with a gleam of nostalgia and a touch of reverence. You know the ones – where you smile and nod, pretending to know exactly what they're talking about. Well, worry no more. By the time you've flipped through these pages, you'll be the one dropping jaws and raising eyebrows with your newfound knowledge.

Ever wondered why your granddad gets misty-eyed talking about Jesse Owens in Berlin, or why your mates can't shut up about Ali vs. Frazier? Maybe you've seen people's faces light up when they recall the Miracle on Ice or gush over the brilliance of Nadia Comaneci's perfect 10. These stories are more than just tales of athletic prowess; they're epic sagas that combine drama, action, and heart – the kind that make you want to stand up and cheer, or maybe even shed a tear.

This book is your golden ticket to the inner circle of sports aficionados. Dive into the jaw-dropping feats of Michael Phelps as he scoops up gold medals like they're going out of style, or feel the electric tension of the 2008 Wimbledon Final where Federer and Nadal went head-to-head in a match for the ages. Discover the underdog triumph of Leicester City's Premier League win and relive the heart-stopping moments of the Boston Red Sox breaking the Curse of the Bambino.

You'll read about the dazzling speed of Usain Bolt, the relentless drive of Serena Williams, and the sheer magic of Tiger Woods at the Masters. These are the stories that have shaped sports history and captured the imagination of fans worldwide. By the time you've soaked up the heroic deeds and legendary matches in these pages, you'll be armed with tales that not only entertain but also inspire.

So sit back, relax, and get ready to be transported into the heart of the action. These stories are the lifeblood of sports lore, the kind of stuff that fuels debates, ignites passions, and builds bridges across generations. Whether you're a die-hard fan or just someone who wants to hold their own in a sports conversation, this book is your ultimate guide. Get ready to amaze your friends and family with your newfound knowledge and perhaps even inspire them to revisit these incredible moments. Happy reading, and welcome to the league of extraordinary sporting legends!

Game Changers: The Greatest Sports Stories Ever Told

Forward 3

Jesse Owens at the 1936 Berlin Olympics 7

Muhammad Ali vs. Joe Frazier - The Fight of the Century (1971) 12

Miracle on Ice (1980 Winter Olympics) 18

Michael Phelps at the 2008 Beijing Olympics 25

Usain Bolt's Triple Triple (2008, 2012, 2016 Olympics) 31

The 1999 Women's World Cup Final 37

Niki Lauda and the 1976 F1 Season 43

Roger Bannister's Four-Minute Mile (1954) 49

Lance Armstrong's Seven Tour de France Wins 54

The Boston Marathon Bombing and Its Aftermath (2013) 60

Diego Maradona's "Hand of God" (1986 World Cup) 67

The 2008 Wimbledon Final - Federer vs. Nadal 72

Tiger Woods' 1997 Masters Victory 77

Babe Ruth's Called Shot (1932 World Series) 82

Jackie Robinson Breaks the Colour Barrier (1947) 88

Jim Thorpe at the 1912 Olympics 94

Pele's World Cup Victories 99

Secretariat's Triple Crown Win (1973) 105

The Immaculate Reception (1972) 110

Nadia Comaneci's Perfect 10 (1976 Olympics) 116

The Battle of the Sexes (1973) 121

Simone Biles' Dominance in Gymnastics 125

Wilt Chamberlain's 100-Point Game (1962) 130

Eric Liddell's 1924 Olympic Gold 135

Michael Jordan's Flu Game (1997 NBA Finals) 140

The New Zealand All Blacks Haka 145

Manchester United's 1999 Treble 150

The Boston Red Sox's 2004 World Series Win 155

Leicester City's Premier League Title (2015-2016) 160

The Rumble in the Jungle (1974) 161

The 2021 Abu Dhabi Grand Prix 165

Leicester City's Premier League Title (2015-2016) 170

The 1994 Olympics: Tonya Harding and Nancy Kerrigan 175

Ford and Ferrari at the 24 Hours of Le Mans 179

Jesse Owens at the 1936 Berlin Olympics

Jesse Owens, born James Cleveland Owens on September 12, 1913, in Oakville, Alabama, was a figure who would rise from humble beginnings to achieve unparalleled success on the world stage. His journey to the 1936 Berlin Olympics, a pivotal moment in sports history, was marked by exceptional talent, relentless determination, and the challenges posed by a deeply divided society. Owens was the youngest of ten children in a sharecropping family, and early on, his family moved to Cleveland, Ohio, as part of the Great Migration. This movement of African Americans from the rural South to the industrial North was driven by the search for better opportunities and escape from the harsh segregation laws of the Jim Crow South.

In Cleveland, Owens attended East Technical High School, where his athletic prowess quickly became evident. Under the guidance of his high school coach, Charles Riley, Owens honed his skills in track and field, setting multiple school records. His remarkable performances caught the attention of college recruiters, and despite numerous offers, he chose to attend Ohio State University. There, he would be coached by Larry Snyder, a former sprinter whose own career had been cut short by injury. Snyder's influence on Owens was profound, helping him refine his technique, improve his stamina, and build the confidence necessary for competition at the highest levels.

The relationship between Owens and Snyder was one of mutual respect and trust, a partnership that would prove crucial in the high-pressure environment of the Olympics. Owens' dedication to his training was evident in his performance at the 1935 Big Ten meet in Ann Arbor, Michigan. In a span of less than an hour, he set three world records and tied a fourth, a feat that remains unmatched. Owens set records in the long jump, 220-yard sprint, and 220-yard low hurdles, and tied the world record for the 100-yard dash. This extraordinary achievement solidified his reputation as one of the greatest athletes of his time and set the stage for his participation in the 1936 Berlin Olympics.

The Berlin Olympics were intended by Adolf Hitler and the Nazi regime to be a showcase for Aryan supremacy. The city was draped in swastikas, and the newly constructed Reich Sports Field was an imposing arena designed to impress and intimidate. Capable of holding 110,000 spectators, the stadium was a grand stage for Hitler's propaganda, projecting an image of German strength and unity. It was within this politically charged atmosphere that Jesse Owens, an African American athlete, would compete, challenging the very ideologies that the Nazi regime sought to promote.

Owens' arrival in Berlin was met with a mix of excitement and tension. He was already a celebrated figure in the athletic world, and his presence at the Games was seen as a direct challenge to the Nazi narrative of racial superiority. Despite the overt racism and segregation he had faced in his own country, Owens was determined to perform at his best and demonstrate the equality of all people through his athletic achievements. The stakes were incredibly high, not just for Owens personally, but for the broader fight against racial discrimination and prejudice.

The opening ceremony of the Berlin Olympics was a grand spectacle, meticulously orchestrated to display the power and organisation of the Nazi regime. Hitler's presence loomed large, his every move closely watched by the international press. For Owens, this was more than just a competition; it was an opportunity to make a powerful statement against the ideologies of hate and division. Despite the hostile environment, Owens remained focused on his goal, drawing strength from his rigorous training and the support of his coach and teammates.

Owens' first event was the 100 metres, a race that demands explosive speed and impeccable timing. The competition was fierce, but Owens, with his characteristic grace and agility, surged ahead, crossing the finish line in 10.3 seconds, equalling the world record. The crowd, a mix of fervent Nazi supporters and international spectators, reacted with a mixture of awe and disbelief. Owens' victory was a direct affront to the Nazi propaganda of Aryan supremacy, a moment that transcended sport and resonated deeply on a political and social level.

His next event, the long jump, presented a different set of challenges. Owens' primary rival was Germany's Luz Long, an athlete who epitomised the Aryan ideal. The tension was palpable as Owens fouled on his first two jumps, putting him in a precarious position. In a remarkable display of sportsmanship, Long approached Owens and suggested he adjust his take-off point to ensure a valid jump. This act of kindness, amidst the charged atmosphere, was a poignant reminder of the unifying spirit of sport. Owens heeded Long's advice and on his final attempt, soared to an Olympic record distance of 8.06 metres, securing the gold medal. The image of Owens and Long celebrating together became one of the enduring symbols of the Games, illustrating a bond that transcended racial and political divides.

Owens' third event, the 200 metres, showcased his versatility and endurance. He dominated the race, finishing in 20.7 seconds, another world record. With three gold medals to his name, Owens had already established himself as one of the greatest athletes in Olympic history. His final event, the 4x100 metre relay, saw him team up with Ralph Metcalfe, Foy Draper, and Frank Wykoff. The American team, already strong, was bolstered by Owens' presence. They set a new world record of 39.8 seconds, with Owens securing his fourth gold medal, a feat that would not be matched until Carl Lewis in 1984.

The aftermath of Owens' victories was a study in contrasts. On one hand, he was celebrated by the international press and hailed as a hero upon his return to the United States. On the other, the racial prejudices of the time reasserted themselves swiftly. Despite his achievements, Owens still faced segregation and discrimination in his own country. Upon his return to New York, he was not allowed to enter through the main doors of the Waldorf Astoria, where a reception was being held in his honour. Instead, he had to use the service entrance, a stark reminder of the systemic racism that pervaded American society.

Owens' post-Olympic life was marked by a series of challenges and setbacks. Despite his unparalleled success at the Games, he struggled to capitalise financially on his achievements. He turned professional, participating in exhibition races and working various jobs to support his family. His attempts to build a career in business met with mixed success, often hampered by the racial barriers of the time. Yet, Owens remained a figure of dignity and inspiration, advocating for the power of sport to transcend racial and political divides.

In addition to his athletic prowess, Owens was known for his humility and grace. He often spoke about the importance of hard work, perseverance, and the support of his family and coach. His relationship with Larry Snyder remained a central part of his story, a testament to the impact that a dedicated and supportive mentor can have on an athlete's career. Owens' bond with Snyder was built on mutual respect and a shared commitment to excellence, qualities that were evident in every aspect of their collaboration.

The 1936 Berlin Olympics were a defining moment in Owens' life, but they were also a significant chapter in the broader history of sport and society. The Games highlighted the potential of sport to challenge and transcend political and social boundaries, offering a glimpse of a world where merit and talent were recognised above race and ideology. Owens' achievements in Berlin were not just athletic triumphs but powerful statements against the ideologies of hatred and division. The setting of the 1936 Olympics, with its blend of grandeur and menace, provided a stark backdrop against which Owens' brilliance shone even brighter.

The characters in Owens' story, from the supportive Larry Snyder to the gracious Luz Long, added depth and nuance to his narrative. Long's act of sportsmanship in the long jump competition was a particularly poignant moment, demonstrating that even in the most charged environments, the spirit of fair play and mutual respect can prevail. Long and Owens' friendship, forged in the heat of competition, was a powerful reminder of the unifying power of sport.

The adversity Owens faced, both on and off the track, highlighted his resilience and strength of character. In an era of profound racial discrimination, Owens' achievements were a beacon of hope and a challenge to the status quo. His victories in Berlin were celebrated around the world, but they also served as a stark contrast to the continued injustices he faced in his own country. Owens' story is a testament to the enduring power of the human spirit to overcome adversity and challenge injustice.

Jesse Owens' legacy is one of profound significance, not just in the realm of sport but in the broader context of social justice and human dignity. His achievements in Berlin were a powerful rebuke to the ideologies of hatred and division that characterised the era

Muhammad Ali vs. Joe Frazier - The Fight of the Century (1971)

The 1971 Muhammad Ali vs. Joe Frazier fight, dubbed the Fight of the Century, was not merely a boxing match but a cultural event that encapsulated the social and political tensions of the time. Muhammad Ali, born Cassius Clay, had become a polarising figure in American society. After converting to Islam and changing his name, he refused induction into the Vietnam War, citing religious beliefs and opposition to the war. This act of defiance led to his boxing licence being revoked, his heavyweight title stripped, and his facing the possibility of imprisonment. For nearly four years, Ali was unable to fight professionally, but he remained a vocal advocate for civil rights and a critic of the war, making him a symbol of resistance and a target of backlash.

Joe Frazier, on the other hand, was a man of few words but tremendous power. Growing up in South Carolina, Frazier moved to Philadelphia, where he honed his skills as a boxer. He emerged as a relentless and ferocious fighter, known for his punishing left hook and unwavering determination. Unlike Ali, Frazier didn't seek the spotlight outside the ring. He was a workmanlike fighter who let his fists do the talking. When Ali was exiled from boxing, Frazier seized the opportunity to rise to the top, becoming the heavyweight champion. Despite his accomplishments, he remained in Ali's shadow, as the world awaited the return of the man who had declared himself "The Greatest."

As Ali battled legal troubles and public opinion, he maintained his physical conditioning and trained in the hopes of a return. When he was finally allowed back into the ring in 1970, he quickly dispatched Jerry

Quarry and Oscar Bonavena, setting the stage for the highly anticipated showdown with Frazier. The fight was scheduled for March 8, 1971, at Madison Square Garden in New York City, the world's most famous arena. The anticipation was palpable, and the bout was billed as the Fight of the Century, a title it would earn in every sense.

The build-up to the fight was intense, with Ali employing his trademark psychological warfare. He ridiculed Frazier, calling him names like "Uncle Tom" and "gorilla," trying to get under his skin and unsettle him. Ali's taunts were relentless and personal, aimed at not just beating Frazier in the ring but breaking his spirit. Frazier, though visibly angered by Ali's insults, remained outwardly stoic and focused. He trained with a single-minded determination, knowing that defeating Ali would solidify his legacy.

The night of the fight, Madison Square Garden was a spectacle. The venue was packed to the rafters with celebrities, politicians, and sports icons, all clamouring to witness history. The atmosphere was electric, a mix of excitement, tension, and anticipation. Ali entered the ring first, exuding confidence and playing to the crowd with his customary bravado. He danced, shadowboxed, and taunted, his every movement a testament to his belief in his own greatness. Frazier entered the ring with a stark contrast in demeanour. He was all business, his face set in a mask of concentration and determination. The fight was a clash of styles as much as personalities, with Ali's grace and speed pitted against Frazier's relentless aggression and power.

From the opening bell, the fight lived up to its billing. Ali started strong, using his reach and footwork to keep Frazier at bay, landing quick jabs and combinations while dancing around the ring. Frazier, however, was undeterred. He pressed forward, bobbing and weaving to get inside Ali's reach, targeting the body with powerful hooks. Ali's strategy was to wear Frazier down, but Frazier's relentless pressure began to take its toll. The contrast in their styles was stark: Ali's elegance and precision versus Frazier's raw power and tenacity.

The middle rounds saw the fight evolve into a gruelling war of attrition. Ali continued to land his jabs and combinations, but Frazier's persistence paid off as he connected with more body shots and hooks. Each punch seemed to chip away at Ali's stamina and resolve. The crowd was on the edge of their seats, each exchange eliciting roars of excitement and anticipation. Ali, ever the showman, continued to taunt and dance, but the strain was showing. Frazier's punches were like sledgehammers, and Ali's legs began to slow. The momentum shifted as Frazier's relentless assault started to wear Ali down.

The ninth round was particularly brutal. Ali, sensing he needed to regain control, came out aggressively, landing several solid punches. Frazier absorbed the blows and responded with a devastating left hook that wobbled Ali. The crowd erupted as Ali stumbled, but he quickly regained his footing and continued to fight back. It was a testament to Ali's resilience and heart, but also to Frazier's power and determination. The rounds that followed were a test of endurance and willpower. Both fighters were exhausted, but neither was willing to give an inch. Ali's face bore the marks of Frazier's relentless assault, while Frazier's relentless pressure showed no signs of abating. The fight became a battle of attrition, with each man digging deep into his reserves of strength and courage.

As the fight entered the championship rounds, the tension was palpable. Ali, recognising the need for a decisive finish, dug deep and launched a series of flurries, trying to overwhelm Frazier with his speed and precision. Frazier, undeterred, kept pressing forward, landing his powerful hooks whenever he got inside. The fifteenth and final round was a microcosm of the entire fight. Both men were exhausted, their bodies battered and bruised, but their spirits unbroken. Ali, despite his fatigue, continued to dance and jab, while Frazier kept moving forward, his left hook finding its mark repeatedly. In the closing moments, Frazier landed a thunderous left hook that sent Ali crashing to the canvas. The crowd erupted as Ali struggled to his feet, a testament to his incredible heart and resilience. He beat the count and continued to fight, but the damage had been done. The final bell rang, and both men, exhausted and battered, stood in the centre of the ring, having given everything they had.

The decision was unanimous. Joe Frazier was declared the winner, retaining his heavyweight title and handing Ali his first professional defeat. The arena erupted in applause and cheers, recognising the incredible effort and skill displayed by both fighters. Frazier had proven himself the undisputed champion, and Ali, despite the loss, had shown the world his heart and courage. The fight was over, but its legacy was just beginning.

In the aftermath, both men would continue their storied careers. Ali would go on to reclaim the heavyweight title and cement his legacy as one of the greatest fighters of all time. Frazier, too, would continue to fight, though his career would be marked by the brutal battles with Ali. Their rivalry would become one of the most storied in sports history, a trilogy of fights that captivated the world and defined an era.

The 1971 fight was more than just a boxing match; it was a cultural event that transcended sports. It was a clash of personalities and ideologies, a symbol of the turbulent times in which it took place. Ali, with his charisma and defiance, represented a new generation that challenged the status quo, while Frazier, with his workmanlike determination, embodied the grit and resilience of the working class.

The fight captured the imagination of the world, and its impact was felt far beyond the confines of the boxing ring.

For Ali, the fight was a pivotal moment in his career. It marked his return to the sport he loved, a chance to prove that he was still the greatest. Despite the loss, Ali's performance against Frazier solidified his place in boxing history. He had faced adversity and emerged with his dignity and spirit intact. The fight also marked a turning point in Ali's public perception. The courage and resilience he displayed in the ring earned him new respect and admiration, even among those who had previously criticised him.

For Frazier, the victory was a defining moment. He had defeated the man many considered unbeatable, proving himself the true heavyweight champion. The win brought him the recognition and respect he deserved, but it also placed him at the centre of one of boxing's greatest rivalries. The animosity between Frazier and Ali would continue, fuelled by their contrasting personalities and the intense battles they fought in the ring.

The Fight of the Century remains a landmark event in the history of sports. It was a night when two of the greatest fighters of all time met in the ring and produced a spectacle that would be remembered for generations. The fight was a testament to the skill, courage, and determination of both men, and it left an indelible mark on the sport of boxing.

As the years passed, the significance of the fight only grew. It became a symbol of the era, reflecting the social and political tensions of the time. Ali and Frazier, through their epic battles, transcended the sport and became cultural icons. Their rivalry, marked by mutual respect and fierce competition, came to epitomise the essence of boxing.

The Fight of the Century was not just about two men trading punches in a ring; it was about the clash of ideologies, the struggle for supremacy, and the unyielding pursuit of greatness. Ali and Frazier gave everything they had, leaving an indelible mark on the sport and the world. Their fight was a testament to the power of the human spirit, the will to overcome adversity, and the enduring legacy of two of the greatest fighters in history.

Miracle on Ice (1980 Winter Olympics)

The Miracle on Ice, the 1980 Winter Olympics ice hockey game between the United States and the Soviet Union, was a moment that transcended sports and became a symbol of hope and perseverance. The backdrop of the Cold War made this more than just a game; it was a clash between two ideologically opposed superpowers, played out on the ice in Lake Placid, New York.

In the late 1970s, the Cold War was at its height. The United States and the Soviet Union were locked in a tense geopolitical standoff that influenced every aspect of life, from politics to culture. Sports were no exception. The Soviet Union's ice hockey team was a powerhouse, dominating international competition for nearly two decades. They were seasoned professionals, often playing together for years, and were considered virtually unbeatable. The Americans, in contrast, were a group of college players, amateurs by the standards of international competition, hastily assembled and given little chance of success.

The U.S. team was coached by Herb Brooks, a man known for his demanding style and unorthodox methods. Brooks, himself a former player who had narrowly missed out on a chance to compete in the Olympics, was determined to mould his young team into a cohesive unit capable of competing with the best in the world. His selection process was rigorous, prioritising not just skill but also the ability to work within a team. Brooks pushed his players to their limits, using psychological tactics to build resilience and unity. His methods were tough, sometimes bordering on brutal, but he believed they were necessary to prepare his team for the monumental challenge ahead.

As the Olympics approached, the U.S. team faced considerable scepticism. Few believed they could stand up to the dominant Soviets, who had won four consecutive gold medals and boasted a roster of the world's best players. The Soviets played a style of hockey that was fast, precise, and ruthlessly efficient. They were disciplined, experienced, and had a level of cohesion that only years of playing together could produce. In contrast, the American team was young, inexperienced, and had only been playing together for a few months. The odds were stacked heavily against them.

The preliminary rounds of the Olympic tournament did little to change the perception of the two teams. The Soviet Union continued to steamroll their opponents, showcasing their superiority with each game. The U.S. team, on the other hand, showed flashes of potential but also moments of vulnerability. They managed to progress through the group stages, but it was clear that if they were to have any chance of winning a medal, they would need to produce something extraordinary.

On February 22, 1980, the stage was set for the semi-final match between the United States and the Soviet Union. The game was held in the Olympic Fieldhouse, a venue that could barely contain the excitement and tension. The crowd was a sea of red, white, and blue, fervently hoping for a miracle but realistically expecting a defeat. The Soviet team, led by their legendary coach Viktor Tikhonov, entered the rink with an air of confidence, almost bordering on arrogance. They had every reason to be confident; they had defeated the Americans 10-3 in a pre-Olympic exhibition game just weeks earlier.

From the first drop of the puck, it was clear that the U.S. team was determined to defy expectations. They played with a level of intensity and cohesion that belied their inexperience. The first period saw the

Soviets dominate possession and chances, but the American team held firm. With just seconds remaining in the period, a stunning goal by Mark Johnson tied the game at 2-2, a crucial moment that gave the U.S. team the belief that they could compete with their formidable opponents.

The second period was a display of defensive grit and goaltending excellence. Jim Craig, the American goalie, was in outstanding form, making save after save to keep his team in the game. The Soviets, frustrated by their inability to pull ahead, replaced their starting goalie, Vladislav Tretiak, with Vladimir Myshkin, a decision that would be widely criticised in the aftermath. Despite their best efforts, the Soviets managed only one goal in the second period, taking a 3-2 lead into the final 20 minutes.

The third period is where the Miracle on Ice truly took shape. The U.S. team, playing with a mixture of desperation and belief, equalised early in the period with a goal from Mark Johnson. The crowd erupted, sensing that something special was happening. Just moments later, team captain Mike Eruzione scored the go-ahead goal, sending the arena into a frenzy. With ten minutes remaining, the Americans clung to their slim lead, knowing that they were on the brink of one of the greatest upsets in sports history.

The final minutes of the game were a test of nerve and endurance. The Soviet team, accustomed to playing with a lead, now found themselves in unfamiliar territory. They pressed forward relentlessly, but the American defence, backed by the brilliant goaltending of Jim Craig, held firm. The clock ticked down agonisingly slowly for the American players and fans, each second bringing them closer to an improbable victory.

When the final buzzer sounded, the arena exploded with joy and disbelief. The U.S. team had defeated the seemingly invincible Soviet Union, 4-3. Players and coaches flooded the ice in celebration, overwhelmed by the magnitude of their achievement. Herb Brooks, who had driven his team with such relentless intensity, was seen in a rare moment of unguarded emotion, tears streaming down his face. The players, many of whom had been playing college hockey just months before, were now Olympic heroes.

The Miracle on Ice was not just a victory for the American team; it was a symbolic triumph that resonated deeply with the nation. At a time when the United States was grappling with economic challenges, political scandals, and the lingering effects of the Vietnam War, the victory provided a much-needed boost to the national spirit. It was a reminder that, even against overwhelming odds, the underdog could prevail.

The game also had significant implications for the sport of ice hockey. It demonstrated that heart, determination, and teamwork could overcome even the most formidable opponents. The American victory inspired a new generation of hockey players and fans, contributing to the growth of the sport in the United States. The Soviet team, though devastated by the loss, would go on to dominate international hockey for years to come, but the memory of their defeat at Lake Placid would linger.

In the years that followed, the players from the 1980 U.S. team went on to various careers, both within and outside of hockey. Some, like Mike Eruzione, embraced their status as national heroes and continued to be involved in the sport as coaches and commentators. Others pursued careers outside of hockey, carrying with them the lessons of teamwork and perseverance they had learned during their Olympic journey. For coach Herb Brooks, the victory cemented his legacy as one of the greatest coaches in hockey history. He continued to coach at various levels, always striving to instil the same values of hard work, discipline, and belief that had driven the Miracle on Ice.

The 1980 Winter Olympics in Lake Placid also featured many other memorable moments and achievements, but the Miracle on Ice stood out as the defining event. It was a moment when sports intersected with politics and culture, creating a story that would be told and retold for generations. The game became a touchstone for discussions about the power of sport to inspire and unite, and a symbol of the enduring appeal of the underdog story.

Looking back, the Miracle on Ice is remembered not just for the final score but for the journey that led to that historic victory. The young American team, led by a visionary coach, overcame doubts and obstacles to achieve something extraordinary. Their victory was a testament to the power of belief, the strength of teamwork, and the magic that can happen when preparation meets opportunity. It remains one of the most iconic moments in sports history, a reminder that, sometimes, the impossible can become possible.

The impact of the Miracle on Ice extended beyond the realm of sports. It became a cultural phenomenon, capturing the imagination of people around the world. The story of the young American underdogs defeating the mighty Soviet machine resonated with audiences far beyond the borders of the United States. It was a story of hope, resilience, and the unyielding spirit of competition. The game has been immortalised in books, documentaries, and films, each retelling capturing the drama and emotion of that fateful night in Lake Placid.

For the players on the U.S. team, the victory was a defining moment in their lives. Many of them went on to have successful careers in the National Hockey League (NHL), but none would ever forget the bond they shared as members of the 1980 Olympic team. The experiences they had, the challenges they overcame, and the triumph they achieved forged lifelong friendships and created a legacy that would endure long after their playing days were over.

Herb Brooks, the architect of the Miracle on Ice, continued to influence the world of hockey long after the 1980 Olympics. His coaching philosophy, which emphasised discipline, teamwork, and mental toughness, became a model for coaches at all levels of the sport. Brooks's ability to motivate and inspire his players was legendary, and his success with the 1980 U.S. team cemented his reputation as one of the greatest coaches in the history of hockey.

The Soviet team, despite their disappointment in 1980, remained a dominant force in international hockey. They continued to win championships and produce some of the greatest players the sport has ever seen. However, the loss to the United States in Lake Placid served as a reminder that even the greatest teams can be vulnerable. It was a humbling experience that underscored the unpredictable nature of sports and the importance of never underestimating an opponent.

The legacy of the Miracle on Ice lives on in the hearts and minds of

those who witnessed it and those who have learned about it in the years since. It is a story that continues to inspire athletes, coaches, and fans around the world. The lessons of perseverance, belief, and the power of teamwork are timeless, and the memory of that incredible game remains a beacon of hope and possibility.

The Miracle on Ice is more than just a moment in sports history; it is a symbol of the enduring human spirit. It reminds us that, no matter the odds, we are capable of achieving greatness when we come together with a common purpose and unwavering belief. The young American team that took to the ice on that February night in 1980 did more than win a hockey game; they created a legacy of inspiration that will be remembered for generations to come.

As we reflect on the Miracle on Ice, we are reminded of the power of sport to bring people together, to inspire hope, and to create moments of magic that transcend time and place. The story of the 1980 U.S. Olympic hockey team is a testament to the strength of the human spirit and the incredible things that can be achieved when we dare to dream and work together to turn those dreams into reality.

Michael Phelps at the 2008 Beijing Olympics

Michael Phelps at the 2008 Beijing Olympics created a spectacle that the world of sports had rarely witnessed. Born in Baltimore, Maryland, in 1985, Phelps began swimming at a young age. His prodigious talent was evident early on, and by the age of 15, he was competing in the 2000 Sydney Olympics, becoming the youngest male to make a U.S. Olympic swim team in 68 years. Though he didn't win a medal, his performance hinted at the extraordinary career that was to follow.

By the time the Beijing Olympics rolled around, Phelps was already a swimming sensation. He had set numerous world records and had won six gold medals and two bronze at the 2004 Athens Olympics. However, Phelps was not content with past glories. His ambition was to surpass the legendary Mark Spitz's record of seven gold medals in a single Olympics, a feat Spitz achieved in Munich in 1972. Phelps's coach, Bob Bowman, was instrumental in this pursuit. Bowman, who had been coaching Phelps since he was 11, designed a rigorous training regimen that pushed Phelps to his limits and honed his technique to near perfection. Their relationship was one of mutual respect and intense dedication, with Bowman often pushing Phelps beyond what he thought possible.

The Beijing National Aquatics Center, known as the Water Cube, was the setting for Phelps's historic run. The state-of-the-art facility, with its unique bubble-like design, was one of the standout venues of the 2008 Games. The atmosphere was electric, with thousands of spectators and millions of viewers worldwide eagerly anticipating each race. The stage was set for Phelps to make history.

Phelps's first event was the 400-meter individual medley. Known for its grueling nature, this event tests a swimmer's versatility and endurance across four different strokes: butterfly, backstroke, breaststroke, and freestyle. Phelps dominated the race from start to finish, breaking his own world record and winning his first gold medal in Beijing. It was a statement performance that set the tone for the rest of the Games.

Next came the 4x100-meter freestyle relay, an event that showcased not just Phelps's talent but also the strength of the American team. The relay was one of the most dramatic races in Olympic history. The French team, boasting the world-record holder in the 100-meter freestyle, Alain Bernard, was favoured to win. However, in a stunning turn of events, American swimmer Jason Lezak swam an extraordinary anchor leg, overtaking Bernard in the final metres to secure the gold for the U.S. team. Phelps, who swam the first leg, watched in amazement as Lezak touched the wall first, securing his second gold medal of the Games.

The 200-meter freestyle, often called the "race of the century," featured a showdown between Phelps and some of the fastest swimmers in the world, including South Korea's Park Tae-hwan and Pieter van den Hoogenband from the Netherlands. Phelps led from start to finish, setting another world record and capturing his third gold medal. His performance was marked by powerful strokes and incredible turns, showcasing his dominance in the pool.

Phelps's next challenge was the 200-meter butterfly, an event where he had already set numerous records. Despite swimming with a water-filled goggle that impaired his vision, Phelps broke his own world record and won his fourth gold medal. His ability to maintain his form and speed under such adverse conditions was a testament to his extraordinary skill and mental toughness.

The 4x200-meter freestyle relay was another opportunity for Phelps to demonstrate his versatility and the strength of the American team. Swimming the lead-off leg, Phelps gave his team a substantial lead, which they never relinquished. The U.S. team set a new world record, and Phelps secured his fifth gold medal. Each victory brought him closer to Spitz's record, and the anticipation continued to build.

In the 200-meter individual medley, Phelps once again showcased his versatility, excelling in all four strokes. He led from the start and finished with another world record, capturing his sixth gold medal. His dominance in this event was evident, as he outpaced his competitors by a significant margin.

The 100-meter butterfly was one of the closest and most dramatic races of Phelps's career. Competing against Serbia's Milorad Čavić, Phelps trailed for most of the race. In the final metres, with an astonishing display of determination and skill, Phelps touched the wall just one-hundredth of a second ahead of Čavić. The photo finish secured Phelps's seventh gold medal, tying Spitz's record. The race was so close that it required extensive review to confirm the result, adding to the drama and excitement.

The final event for Phelps was the 4x100-meter medley relay. Swimming the butterfly leg, Phelps helped the U.S. team to another world record and his eighth gold medal, breaking Spitz's long-standing record. The achievement was monumental, cementing Phelps's status as the greatest swimmer of all time. His eight gold medals in a single Olympics were unprecedented, and his performances in Beijing were nothing short of extraordinary.

Phelps's success in Beijing was not just a result of his natural talent but also his unparalleled work ethic and dedication. His training regimen was famously intense, often involving multiple workouts a day and covering miles in the pool. His diet, too, was a topic of fascination, as he consumed an enormous number of calories to fuel his rigorous training. Phelps's mental preparation was also crucial, as he visualised each race and focused on his goals with unyielding determination.

The Beijing Olympics were a culmination of years of hard work, sacrifice, and relentless pursuit of excellence. Phelps's achievements were celebrated around the world, and he became a global icon. His performances inspired a new generation of swimmers and athletes, showing what could be achieved with dedication and perseverance.

Phelps's journey to Beijing was not without its challenges. He faced numerous obstacles, including injuries and the pressure of immense expectations. In 2007, he fractured his wrist in a freak accident, which could have derailed his preparation for the Olympics. However, Phelps's resilience and determination saw him recover quickly and return to peak form. He also had to contend with the scrutiny and pressure of being the face of the U.S. Olympic team, with the media and public expecting nothing less than perfection.

Phelps's relationship with his coach, Bob Bowman, was a crucial factor in his success. Bowman's demanding and often unconventional coaching methods pushed Phelps to his limits and brought out the best in him. Their partnership was built on trust and mutual respect, with Bowman understanding how to motivate Phelps and channel his extraordinary talent. Bowman's role in Phelps's success cannot be overstated, as he was the architect behind Phelps's training and race strategies.

The support of Phelps's family was also instrumental. His mother, Debbie Phelps, was a constant presence and source of encouragement. She had supported him throughout his career, attending his competitions and providing the emotional support needed to navigate the highs and lows of elite sport. Phelps often credited his family with helping him stay grounded and focused, even amidst the intense pressures of international competition.

The Beijing Olympics were a landmark event not just for Phelps but for the sport of swimming. His performances captivated audiences worldwide and brought unprecedented attention to the sport. The Water Cube, with its distinctive architecture and state-of-the-art facilities, provided a fitting stage for Phelps's historic achievements. The atmosphere in the venue was electric, with spectators and fellow athletes alike recognising the significance of what they were witnessing.

Phelps's impact extended beyond the pool. His success in Beijing made him a global superstar, and he used his platform to promote swimming and encourage young people to get involved in the sport. He also became an advocate for water safety and worked with various charitable organisations to promote healthy lifestyles and the importance of physical activity. His influence extended far beyond his medal count, as he inspired countless individuals to pursue their dreams and strive for excellence.

In the years following Beijing, Phelps continued to compete at the highest level, adding to his already impressive medal tally at subsequent World Championships and Olympics. However, the 2008 Games remained the pinnacle of his career, a testament to what can be achieved through talent, hard work, and unwavering determination. Phelps's eight gold medals in Beijing stand as a monumental achievement, a record that may never be broken.

The legacy of Michael Phelps at the 2008 Beijing Olympics is one of inspiration and greatness. His performances were a masterclass in athletic excellence, showcasing the peak of human potential. The story of his journey to Beijing, the challenges he overcame, and the triumphs he achieved will be remembered as one of the greatest chapters in the history of sport. Phelps's name became synonymous with swimming excellence, and his legacy continues to inspire athletes around the world to dream big and pursue their goals with passion and dedication.

His journey is a testament to the strength of the human spirit and the incredible things that can be achieved when talent, hard work, and determination come together. The 2008 Beijing Olympics will forever be remembered as the stage where Michael Phelps etched his name into the annals of sporting history, achieving a level of greatness that few can ever hope to attain.

Usain Bolt's Triple Triple (2008, 2012, 2016 Olympics)

Usain Bolt's Triple Triple—winning gold medals in the 100 meters, 200 meters, and 4x100 meters relay at three consecutive Olympics—is one of the most extraordinary achievements in the history of athletics. This feat, accomplished at the 2008 Beijing Olympics, the 2012 London Olympics, and the 2016 Rio de Janeiro Olympics, solidified Bolt's status as the fastest man alive and an icon of the sport. Born in Jamaica in 1986, Usain Bolt's journey to Olympic stardom was marked by incredible talent, rigorous training, and a charismatic personality that endeared him to fans around the world.

Before Bolt's Olympic success, his potential was evident from a young age. Growing up in Trelawny, Jamaica, Bolt was passionate about sports, excelling in cricket and football. His sprinting talent was discovered by his primary school coaches, who noticed his exceptional speed. By the age of 15, Bolt had already made a name for himself on the world stage, winning the 200 meters at the World Junior Championships in 2002. Despite his early success, Bolt's career was not without challenges. He faced injuries and setbacks, which hindered his progress and raised doubts about his ability to compete at the highest level.

The 2008 Beijing Olympics marked Bolt's arrival on the global stage. The Bird's Nest stadium, with its iconic architecture, provided the perfect backdrop for his historic performance. In the 100 meters final, Bolt's confidence was palpable. He started the race with a slightly sluggish reaction time, but his acceleration was unmatched. As he approached the finish line, Bolt glanced to his sides and pounded his chest in celebration, crossing the line in 9.69 seconds, setting a new world record. This performance was not only a display of his incredible speed but also his charisma and showmanship, which captivated audiences worldwide.

In the 200 meters, Bolt continued his dominance. He ran a perfect race, breaking Michael Johnson's 12-year-old world record with a time of 19.30 seconds. His long strides and smooth running style were on full display, and his margin of victory left no doubt about his superiority. The 4x100 meters relay was the final event of Bolt's Beijing campaign. Teaming up with his Jamaican teammates, Bolt ran the third leg, extending their lead before Asafa Powell anchored them to victory. The team set a new world record, completing Bolt's first Triple Triple.

The 2012 London Olympics were a chance for Bolt to defend his titles and cement his legacy. The atmosphere in the Olympic Stadium was electric, with fans eager to witness another Bolt masterclass. In the 100 meters final, Bolt faced strong competition from compatriot Yohan Blake, who had beaten him at the Jamaican trials. Despite a less-than-ideal start, Bolt powered through the field, winning the race in 9.63 seconds, another Olympic record. His victory was a testament to his ability to perform under pressure and his unrivalled sprinting prowess.

The 200 meters saw Bolt once again dominate. He crossed the finish line in 19.32 seconds, becoming the first man to win back-to-back Olympic titles in both the 100 and 200 meters. His celebrations were joyous, as he revelled in his achievements and the adulation of the crowd. The 4x100 meters relay was a fitting finale to Bolt's London campaign. Running the anchor leg, Bolt brought the Jamaican team home in a world record time of 36.84 seconds, completing his second Triple Triple and reinforcing his status as the king of sprints.

By the time the 2016 Rio de Janeiro Olympics arrived, Bolt was already a legend. Yet, he faced new challenges, including injuries and the emergence of younger competitors. Despite these obstacles, Bolt's determination and confidence never wavered. In the 100 meters final, he once again proved his mettle. With a typically powerful start and a blistering finish, Bolt crossed the line in 9.81 seconds, securing his third consecutive Olympic gold in the event. His joy and relief were evident as he celebrated with his trademark lightning bolt pose.

The 200 meters in Rio saw Bolt aiming for another historic achievement. He won the race comfortably, finishing in 19.78 seconds. While he did not break his own world record, his victory was nonetheless a remarkable achievement, as he became the first athlete to win three consecutive Olympic golds in the 200 meters. Bolt's celebration was a mix of elation and nostalgia, as he acknowledged that this would be his final Olympic appearance in the event.

The 4x100 meters relay was Bolt's final Olympic race. The Jamaican team, including Asafa Powell, Yohan Blake, and Nickel Ashmeade, were determined to send Bolt off with another gold. Bolt ran the anchor leg, bringing the team home in 37.27 seconds. The victory completed his third Triple Triple, a feat unparalleled in the history of athletics. Bolt's farewell to the Olympics was emotional, as he soaked in the applause and admiration of fans worldwide.

Bolt's journey to the Triple Triple was not just about his physical abilities but also his mental strength and resilience. Throughout his career, he faced numerous challenges, including injuries and the pressure of maintaining his dominance. His training regimen, under the guidance of coach Glen Mills, was intense and meticulously planned. Mills played a crucial role in Bolt's development, helping him refine his technique and maximise his potential. Bolt's success was also a result of his natural talent and his unique physiology. Standing at 6 feet 5 inches tall, his long legs gave him a significant advantage in stride length, allowing him to cover more ground with each step. His combination of speed, strength, and coordination was unmatched, making him a formidable competitor.

Off the track, Bolt's charismatic personality and sense of humour endeared him to fans and media alike. He was known for his playful antics, such as pretending to play the violin before races or striking his famous lightning bolt pose. These traits made him a beloved figure, transcending the sport and becoming a global icon. Bolt's success also had a significant impact on Jamaican athletics. His achievements inspired a new generation of sprinters, contributing to the country's continued dominance in sprinting events. Athletes like Yohan Blake, Shelly-Ann Fraser-Pryce, and Elaine Thompson-Herah followed in Bolt's footsteps, maintaining Jamaica's reputation as a sprinting powerhouse

Bolt's legacy extends beyond his records and medals. He has become a symbol of excellence and perseverance, demonstrating that greatness is achieved through hard work, dedication, and a passion for one's craft. His influence can be seen in the aspirations of young athletes around the world, who look up to him as a role model. The impact of Bolt's Triple Triple is also evident in the broader context of athletics. His performances brought unprecedented attention to the sport, drawing in new fans and increasing its popularity. Bolt's ability to captivate audiences with his speed and charisma revitalised interest in track and field, making it one of the highlights of the Olympic Games.

In retirement, Bolt has continued to be involved in sports and entertainment. He pursued a brief career in professional football, playing for clubs like Central Coast Mariners in Australia. While his football career did not reach the heights of his sprinting achievements, it showcased his willingness to embrace new challenges and continue pushing his limits. Bolt has also been active in charitable work, using his platform to support various causes. His Usain Bolt Foundation aims to benefit children and young people, providing educational and cultural opportunities to those in need. Bolt's commitment to giving back reflects his understanding of the impact he can have beyond the track.

The story of Usain Bolt's Triple Triple is a testament to the power of determination, talent, and the pursuit of excellence. His journey from a young boy in Jamaica to the fastest man in the world is a source of inspiration for millions. Bolt's achievements in Beijing, London, and Rio de Janeiro will forever be remembered as some of the greatest moments in Olympic history. As we look back on Bolt's career, we are reminded of the joy and excitement he brought to the sport. His electrifying performances, charismatic personality, and unwavering commitment to greatness set him apart as one of the most iconic athletes of all time. Bolt's legacy is not just defined by his records but by the impact he has had on the world of sports and beyond. The Triple Triple stands as a symbol of what can be achieved when talent, hard work, and passion come together. Bolt's name will be forever etched in the annals of athletics, a reminder of the incredible heights that can be reached when one dares to dream and works tirelessly to turn those dreams into reality.

Usain Bolt's journey is also a testament to the power of sports to bring people together. His performances transcended national boundaries and cultural differences, uniting fans around the world in admiration and awe. Bolt's ability to connect with audiences and inspire them with his achievements made him a global ambassador for the sport and a beacon of hope and possibility. As we reflect on the legacy of Usain Bolt, we celebrate not only his unparalleled success on the track but also the spirit of joy and enthusiasm he brought to the sport. Bolt's story is one of triumph over adversity, the pursuit of excellence, and the power of believing in oneself. His Triple Triple will continue to inspire future generations of athletes, reminding them that with hard work, dedication, and a bit of flair, anything is possible.

In the annals of Olympic history, Usain Bolt's name will forever stand out as a symbol of greatness. His journey from a young Jamaican sprinter to the fastest man on earth is a story of perseverance, talent, and the relentless pursuit of excellence. The Triple Triple is not just an athletic achievement; it is a testament to the power of dreams and the extraordinary things that can be achieved when one dares to dream big and works tirelessly to make those dreams a reality.

The 1999 Women's World Cup Final

The 1999 Women's World Cup Final was a landmark event in the history of football, transcending the sport to become a cultural phenomenon. Held at the Rose Bowl in Pasadena, California, the final between the United States and China was a culmination of years of dedication, struggle, and triumph for women's football. This event was not just a match but a statement about the growing prominence and acceptance of women's sports on a global stage.

In the years leading up to the 1999 Women's World Cup, women's football had been fighting for recognition and respect. The sport was often overshadowed by its male counterpart, receiving far less media attention and financial support. However, the success of the U.S. women's national team in the 1991 Women's World Cup, where they emerged as champions, began to change perceptions. This victory, combined with the team's gold medal win at the 1996 Atlanta Olympics, helped build a strong foundation for the growth of women's football in the United States.

The 1999 Women's World Cup was a chance for the sport to showcase its development and attract a larger audience. The tournament was held in the United States, with matches spread across various cities, reflecting the organisers' ambition to promote the game nationwide. The decision to hold the final at the Rose Bowl, a stadium with a capacity of over 90,000, was a bold move, signalling confidence in the sport's drawing power. As the tournament progressed, it became clear that this confidence was well-placed.

The United States women's national team entered the tournament as favourites, bolstered by their previous successes and a squad brimming with talent. Key players like Mia Hamm, known for her speed and skill, and Kristine Lilly, a versatile and reliable midfielder, were central to the team's strategy. Goalkeeper Briana Scurry provided a formidable last line of defence, while defenders like Joy Fawcett and Carla Overbeck brought experience and leadership to the backline. The team was coached by Tony DiCicco, whose tactical acumen and ability to motivate his players were critical to their success.

The tournament saw the U.S. team dominate their group stage matches, displaying a blend of attacking flair and defensive solidity. Victories against Denmark, Nigeria, and North Korea set the stage for a quarter-final clash with Germany. This match was a hard-fought encounter, with the U.S. emerging victorious thanks to goals from Tiffeny Milbrett and Brandi Chastain. The semi-final against Brazil was another stern test, but the Americans prevailed with a 2-0 win, setting up a highly anticipated final against China.

China, known for their disciplined and technically proficient play, were formidable opponents. The team featured star players like Sun Wen, a prolific striker with a keen eye for goal, and Liu Ailing, a creative midfielder capable of dictating the tempo of the game. Their journey to the final was marked by impressive performances, including a resounding 5-0 victory over Norway in the semi-final. Coached by Ma Liangxing, China were tactically astute and well-prepared, setting the stage for an epic showdown.

The final on July 10, 1999, drew a record crowd of 90,185 spectators to the Rose Bowl, the largest attendance ever for a women's sporting event. The atmosphere was electric, with fans eagerly anticipating a clash between two of the best teams in the world. The match itself was a tense and closely contested affair, reflecting the high stakes and the quality of both sides.

From the outset, the U.S. and China battled fiercely for control of the game. The Americans, driven by the vocal home support, pressed forward with relentless energy. Mia Hamm and Tiffeny Milbrett spearheaded the attack, constantly probing the Chinese defence. However, China's backline, marshalled by the experienced Wen Lirong, held firm. The midfield battle was equally intense, with Kristine Lilly and Julie Foudy working tirelessly to disrupt China's rhythm and create opportunities for their forwards.

China, for their part, showcased their technical prowess and composure on the ball. Sun Wen was a constant threat, using her speed and intelligence to exploit spaces in the American defence. Liu Ailing orchestrated play from midfield, her precise passing and vision creating several dangerous moments. Despite the end-to-end action, both defences stood strong, and the first half ended goalless.

As the second half progressed, the tension in the stadium grew palpable. Both teams had chances to break the deadlock, but outstanding performances from the goalkeepers, Briana Scurry for the U.S. and Gao Hong for China, kept the score level. Scurry's reflex saves and command of the penalty area were crucial, while Gao Hong's agility and shot-stopping abilities frustrated the American forwards.

With the match still tied at 0-0 after 90 minutes, the game went into extra time. The intensity and physicality of the contest increased, as both teams pushed for a decisive goal. Fatigue began to set in, but the players' determination and resilience were evident. The Americans continued to press, with Shannon MacMillan's pace causing problems for the Chinese defence. China, however, remained dangerous on the counter-attack, with Sun Wen and Liu Ailing combining well to create openings.

The defining moment of the match came in the dying minutes of extra time. A corner kick from the right was met by a powerful header from Kristine Lilly, only for Chinese defender Fan Yunjie to clear the ball off the line. The near miss encapsulated the drama and tension of the game, as both teams came agonisingly close to scoring.

With the score still 0-0 after extra time, the final was decided by a penalty shootout. The Rose Bowl fell silent as the players prepared for the nerve-wracking ordeal. The U.S. were up first, and Carla Overbeck stepped up to take the opening penalty. She calmly slotted the ball past Gao Hong, giving the Americans a crucial early lead. China responded with a successful penalty from Liu Ying, levelling the score.

The shootout continued with both teams converting their penalties. Mia Hamm, Joy Fawcett, and Kristine Lilly all scored for the U.S., while Sun Wen, Pu Wei, and Fan Yunjie did the same for China. The pressure mounted as the shootout progressed, with each penalty carrying the weight of a nation's hopes.

The pivotal moment came when Liu Ailing stepped up to take China's fourth penalty. Her shot was saved by Briana Scurry, who dived to her left to make a crucial stop. The save gave the U.S. the advantage, and they capitalised on it. Brandi Chastain, known for her composure under pressure, stepped forward to take the final penalty. Chastain's strike was powerful and precise, finding the back of the net and securing victory for the United States.

The scenes of celebration that followed were unforgettable. Brandi Chastain, in a moment of pure elation, whipped off her jersey and fell to her knees, her arms raised in triumph. The image of Chastain in her sports bra became iconic, symbolising the joy and empowerment of women's sport. Her celebration was not just a personal moment of victory but a powerful statement about the significance of the win for women's football.

The U.S. players were mobbed by their teammates and coaches, the joy and relief palpable. The crowd erupted in cheers, the atmosphere one of unbridled celebration. The victory was a testament to the hard work, dedication, and resilience of the U.S. team, who had overcome formidable opponents and immense pressure to emerge as world champions.

The impact of the 1999 Women's World Cup Final extended far beyond the confines of the Rose Bowl. The match was broadcast to millions of viewers around the world, bringing unprecedented attention to women's football. The success of the tournament and the thrilling final helped to elevate the sport's profile and inspire a new generation of female athletes.

For the players, the victory was a career-defining moment. Mia Hamm, already a global superstar, cemented her legacy as one of the greatest footballers of all time. Her skill, speed, and leadership were instrumental in the U.S. team's success. Kristine Lilly, with her tireless work rate and versatility, was another key figure, her contributions vital in both defence and attack. Briana Scurry's heroics in goal were crucial, her saves in the shootout a defining factor in the victory.

The triumph also had a significant impact on women's sports in the United States. The visibility and success of the U.S. team inspired increased investment and interest in women's football, leading to the establishment of professional leagues and the growth of youth programmes. The legacy of the 1999 Women's World Cup Final continues to influence the sport today, as more opportunities and resources are made available to female athletes.

China's performance in the tournament and the final was also commendable. The team showcased their skill, discipline, and tactical acumen, pushing the U.S. to their limits. Players like Sun Wen and Liu Ailing were outstanding, their talent and determination earning them respect and admiration. Despite the disappointment of losing the final, China's campaign in the 1999 Women's World Cup was a testament to their quality and a significant moment in the history of women's football.

The 1999 Women's World Cup Final remains one of the most iconic moments in sports history. It was a match that transcended football, capturing the imagination of fans and inspiring a new generation of female athletes. The U.S. team's victory was a triumph of skill, determination, and resilience, and its impact continues to be felt today. The legacy of that historic final is a testament to the power of sport to inspire, unite, and empower people around the world.

The 1999 Women's World Cup Final will forever be remembered not just for the thrilling match and the dramatic penalty shootout but for what it represented: the rise of women's football and the breaking down of barriers in sports. The match at the Rose Bowl was a celebration of talent, hard work, and the unyielding spirit of female athletes, and its significance continues to resonate across the sporting world.

Niki Lauda and the 1976 F1 Season

Niki Lauda's 1976 accident and subsequent recovery and return to Formula 1 racing are among the most dramatic and inspiring stories in the history of the sport. Born on February 22, 1949, in Vienna, Austria, Andreas Nikolaus Lauda, better known as Niki, was destined for greatness in motorsport. From an early age, Lauda demonstrated a natural talent and passion for racing, which eventually led him to the pinnacle of Formula 1.

By the mid-1970s, Lauda had established himself as one of the top drivers in Formula 1. Driving for Ferrari, he won the World Championship in 1975 and was leading the 1976 championship by a comfortable margin as the season reached its midpoint. Lauda's driving style was characterised by precision, intelligence, and a deep understanding of the mechanics of his car. His technical knowledge and ability to communicate effectively with his engineers made him a formidable competitor.

The 1976 season was shaping up to be another successful campaign for Lauda. Ferrari had provided him with a competitive car, the 312T2, and Lauda's performances on the track were consistently impressive. His main rival that season was James Hunt, a British driver known for his aggressive style and charismatic personality. The rivalry between Lauda and Hunt added an extra layer of drama to the season, capturing the attention of fans worldwide.

The German Grand Prix at the Nürburgring, held on August 1, 1976, was a pivotal moment in the championship. The Nürburgring, often referred to as the "Green Hell," was one of the most challenging and dangerous circuits in the world. Its long, winding layout, combined with unpredictable weather conditions, made it a true test of skill and bravery for any driver. Despite reservations about the safety of the track, the race went ahead as planned.

Lauda, always conscious of the dangers inherent in motorsport, had voiced his concerns about the safety of the Nürburgring. Nevertheless, he took to the track, determined to maintain his lead in the championship. As the race began, the conditions were difficult, with rain making the already treacherous circuit even more hazardous. On the second lap, disaster struck. Lauda's Ferrari hit a barrier, bounced back onto the track, and burst into flames.

The scene was horrifying. Trapped in the burning wreckage, Lauda suffered severe burns to his face and head, and inhaled toxic fumes that damaged his lungs. Fellow drivers Arturo Merzario, Guy Edwards, Brett Lunger, and Harald Ertl stopped their cars and rushed to Lauda's aid, pulling him from the inferno. Their bravery undoubtedly saved Lauda's life, but his injuries were life-threatening.

Lauda was airlifted to a nearby hospital, where he was given the last rites by a priest. His condition was critical, and the prognosis was grim. Lauda's family, friends, and the motorsport community braced themselves for the worst. Yet, against all odds, Lauda began to show signs of recovery. His determination and willpower, traits that had served him well on the track, now played a crucial role in his fight for survival.

The road to recovery was long and arduous. Lauda underwent multiple surgeries to repair the damage to his face and scalp. The burns had left him with extensive scarring, and he had to wear a specially designed cap to protect his healing skin. The inhalation of toxic fumes had severely affected his lungs, making breathing difficult and painful.

Despite the physical and emotional toll, Lauda's resolve never wavered. He was determined not only to survive but to return to the sport he loved.

Incredibly, just six weeks after his accident, Lauda made a miraculous return to Formula 1 at the Italian Grand Prix in Monza. His comeback was nothing short of extraordinary. Lauda's face was still heavily bandaged, and he was far from fully recovered. Yet, his competitive spirit and determination to race again pushed him back into the cockpit of his Ferrari. The motorsport world watched in awe as Lauda lined up on the grid, ready to compete.

Lauda's performance at Monza was a testament to his incredible courage and skill. Despite the pain and discomfort, he finished fourth, an astonishing achievement given the circumstances. The sight of Lauda back in his car, defying the odds, was an inspiration to fans and fellow drivers alike. His return was a reminder of the resilience and indomitable spirit that define true champions.

The championship battle between Lauda and Hunt resumed, with the rivalry reaching its peak. Lauda's remarkable recovery and return to racing added a new dimension to the contest. Each race was a test of physical endurance and mental fortitude for Lauda, but he continued to compete at the highest level. The season culminated in a dramatic showdown at the Japanese Grand Prix at Fuji Speedway.

The conditions at Fuji were treacherous, with heavy rain making the track extremely dangerous. Lauda, still recovering and concerned for his safety, made the difficult decision to withdraw from the race after just two laps. Hunt, meanwhile, battled through the conditions to finish third, securing enough points to win the championship by a single point. Lauda's decision to prioritise his safety and well-being was a testament to his wisdom and maturity as a driver.

Despite losing the championship, Lauda's heroics throughout the 1976 season earned him immense respect and admiration. His determination to return to racing and his ability to compete at the highest level, despite the odds, cemented his status as one of the greatest drivers in the history of the sport. Lauda's journey from the brink of death to the podium at Monza remains one of the most inspiring stories in motorsport.

Lauda continued to race in Formula 1, winning two more World Championships in 1977 and 1984. His success on the track was matched by his contributions off it. Lauda became a prominent figure in the motorsport world, known for his insights and expertise. He took on various roles, including team management and advisory positions, and his influence on the sport remained significant long after his retirement from racing.

Niki Lauda's legacy extends beyond his achievements on the track. His story is one of resilience, determination, and the human spirit's ability to overcome seemingly insurmountable challenges. Lauda's courage in the face of adversity and his unwavering passion for racing continue to inspire generations of drivers and fans. His remarkable journey from the flames of the Nürburgring to the heights of Formula 1 glory is a testament to the enduring power of hope, perseverance, and the pursuit of excellence.

The impact of Lauda's story is felt not only in the world of motorsport but also in popular culture. His life and career have been the subject of numerous books, documentaries, and films, including the critically acclaimed movie "Rush," directed by Ron Howard. The film, which chronicles the rivalry between Lauda and Hunt, brought Lauda's story to a new audience, highlighting the extraordinary nature of his achievements.

Lauda's influence on Formula 1 continues to be felt today. His approach to racing, characterised by a combination of technical expertise and mental toughness, set a standard for future generations of drivers. Lauda's commitment to safety, born out of his own harrowing experiences, played a crucial role in advancing safety measures within the sport. His legacy is one of innovation, excellence, and the relentless pursuit of improvement.

The Nürburgring crash in 1976 was a pivotal moment in Lauda's life and career, but it did not define him. Instead, it highlighted his remarkable character and his ability to rise above adversity. Lauda's recovery and return to racing were not just about physical healing; they were about demonstrating the strength of the human spirit and the power of determination.

Niki Lauda's story is a celebration of resilience, courage, and the enduring passion for racing. His journey from the devastating crash at the Nürburgring to his triumphant return to Formula 1 is a powerful reminder of what can be achieved through sheer will and determination. Lauda's legacy continues to inspire and captivate, ensuring that his place in the annals of motorsport history remains secure. His remarkable life and career are a testament to the extraordinary heights that can be reached when one refuses to give up, no matter the obstacles in the way.

Roger Bannister's Four-Minute Mile (1954)

Roger Bannister's historic four-minute mile in 1954 was a seminal moment in sports history, encapsulating human perseverance, scientific training, and sheer willpower. Bannister, a medical student at the time, balanced his rigorous academic schedule with an intense training regimen, aiming to break what was considered the ultimate barrier in middle-distance running. Born in 1929 in Harrow, England, Bannister was an exceptional student who gravitated towards athletics at a young age. His passion for running blossomed during his time at Oxford University, where he began to focus on the mile as his event of choice.

The four-minute mile had long been regarded as an insurmountable barrier, a feat that many believed was beyond human capability. The best runners of the time, despite their efforts, seemed unable to break the elusive mark, leading to widespread speculation that it was physiologically impossible. This belief only added to the mystique and allure of the challenge. Bannister, however, was undeterred by such notions. His approach to training was scientific, informed by his medical studies and a deep understanding of human physiology. He believed that with the right combination of physical preparation and mental fortitude, the barrier could be broken

Bannister's path to the record was not without its challenges. He faced intense competition from runners like John Landy of Australia, who was also vying to be the first to break the four-minute barrier. Landy, a formidable runner, had come tantalisingly close to the mark, fuelling a fierce rivalry between the two athletes. Bannister's training regimen was meticulously planned, incorporating interval training and careful monitoring of his physical condition. He was coached by Franz Stampfl, whose innovative methods played a crucial role in Bannister's preparation. Stampfl emphasised the importance of pacing and mental resilience, helping Bannister to hone his strategy for the historic run.

The setting for Bannister's record attempt was the Iffley Road Track in Oxford, a modest venue that would soon become legendary. The date was set for May 6, 1954, a day that would go down in history. Bannister was supported by his friends and fellow athletes, Chris Brasher and Chris Chataway, who would act as pacemakers during the race. Their role was critical, as maintaining the right pace was essential for Bannister to achieve his goal. The weather on the day of the attempt was far from ideal, with winds threatening to derail the effort. However, as the start time approached, the wind subsided, and conditions improved.

The race itself was a masterclass in pacing and strategy. Brasher led the first lap, setting a steady pace that allowed Bannister to conserve his energy. As they completed the first lap in just under 58 seconds, the plan was unfolding perfectly. Bannister stayed close behind, his focus unwavering. On the second lap, Brasher continued to lead, maintaining the pace, while Bannister remained composed, his breathing controlled and his strides efficient. As they approached the halfway mark, the time was 1:58, precisely on target. Chataway then took over the pacing duties, leading Bannister through the crucial third lap.

The third lap was where the mental and physical demands intensified. Bannister had to resist the urge to surge too early, conserving his energy for the final push. Chataway's pacing was crucial, keeping Bannister on track despite the mounting fatigue. They completed the third lap in 3:01, setting the stage for the dramatic final lap. With 300 yards to go, Bannister made his move, accelerating past Chataway and into the history books. His final sprint was a display of sheer determination and speed, as he crossed the finish line in 3:59.4, shattering the four-minute barrier.

The crowd erupted in celebration, aware that they had witnessed a historic moment. Bannister, exhausted but elated, had achieved what many had deemed impossible. His time of 3:59.4 was not just a record but a testament to human potential and the power of perseverance. The impact of Bannister's achievement was profound, inspiring athletes around the world and redefining the limits of human endurance.

In the aftermath of the record-breaking run, Bannister's life changed dramatically. He became a global icon, celebrated for his incredible achievement and his contributions to the sport. However, Bannister remained humble, continuing his medical studies and pursuing a career in neurology. His focus shifted from athletics to medicine, where he made significant contributions to the field.

The significance of Bannister's four-minute mile extended beyond the realm of athletics. It represented a triumph of human spirit and the relentless pursuit of excellence. His approach to training, combining scientific principles with rigorous practice, set a new standard for athletes and coaches alike. Bannister's achievement also highlighted the importance of mental resilience and strategic planning in overcoming seemingly insurmountable challenges.

The rivalry between Bannister and John Landy continued to captivate the athletic world. Landy, inspired by Bannister's success, broke the four-minute barrier shortly after, running a time of 3:57.9. Their rivalry culminated in a memorable race at the 1954 Commonwealth Games in Vancouver, known as the "Miracle Mile." Both runners broke the four-minute mark in that race, with Bannister narrowly edging out Landy to win.

Bannister's legacy in athletics is enduring. His historic run at Iffley Road Track remains a symbol of human achievement and the power of determination. The four-minute mile, once considered an unattainable goal, became a benchmark for middle-distance runners, inspiring generations of athletes to push the boundaries of what is possible. Bannister's influence extended beyond his own achievements, as he became a mentor and inspiration for aspiring runners and coaches.

The impact of Bannister's four-minute mile was felt across the world of sports. It demonstrated the importance of combining scientific knowledge with athletic training, a concept that has since become a cornerstone of modern sports science. Bannister's approach to training, with its emphasis on pacing, interval work, and mental preparation, influenced countless athletes and coaches, shaping the way middle-distance running is approached to this day.

Bannister's contribution to athletics was not limited to his record-breaking run. He was an advocate for the sport, promoting the values of dedication, perseverance, and fair play. His humility and sportsmanship set an example for others, and his commitment to excellence extended beyond the track. Bannister's achievements in both athletics and medicine are a testament to his extraordinary talent and determination.

The story of Roger Bannister's four-minute mile is one of triumph over adversity, a reminder that with hard work, determination, and the right support, even the most daunting challenges can be overcome. Bannister's journey from a young athlete with a dream to a global icon is a source of inspiration for anyone striving to achieve their goals. His legacy continues to inspire and motivate, reminding us of the incredible potential of the human spirit.

Lance Armstrong's Seven Tour de France Wins

Lance Armstrong's seven Tour de France wins stand as one of the most compelling and controversial stories in the world of professional cycling. Born in 1971 in Texas, Armstrong showed exceptional athletic talent from a young age. He began his sporting career as a triathlete before focusing on cycling, where his potential quickly became apparent. His aggressive racing style and natural endurance set him apart from his peers, propelling him into the professional ranks at a young age.

Armstrong's early career was marked by promise and potential. He won the World Championship in 1993 and performed well in various European races. However, his career trajectory took a dramatic turn in 1996 when he was diagnosed with advanced testicular cancer. The cancer had spread to his lungs, abdomen, and brain, and his prognosis was grim. Despite the severe diagnosis, Armstrong underwent aggressive treatment, including surgery and chemotherapy, and displayed an extraordinary will to survive. His recovery was nothing short of miraculous, and within a year, he was back on his bike, determined to return to professional cycling.

Armstrong's comeback was marked by a renewed focus and determination. He joined the U.S. Postal Service team, and his preparation for the Tour de France became obsessive. Armstrong and his team meticulously planned their strategy, incorporating the latest in sports science, training methods, and equipment technology. His coach, Chris Carmichael, and team director, Johan Bruyneel, played crucial roles in shaping his training regimen and race tactics.

The 1999 Tour de France marked Armstrong's return to the grand stage of professional cycling. The race started in Puy du Fou, a medieval-themed amusement park in France, and Armstrong immediately made his presence felt. The early stages saw him staying close to the front, conserving energy and avoiding crashes. The turning point came during the first mountain stage in the Pyrenees, where Armstrong launched a decisive attack, leaving his rivals behind. His climbing prowess and time-trialling abilities were on full display as he secured the yellow jersey, the symbol of the race leader, for the first time. Armstrong's victory was seen as a triumph of the human spirit, overcoming his near-fatal illness to win the most prestigious race in cycling.

The following years saw Armstrong dominate the Tour de France, winning consecutive titles from 2000 to 2005. Each victory was built on meticulous preparation, a strong team, and Armstrong's unparalleled mental and physical resilience. The 2000 Tour saw him battling the challenging climbs of Mont Ventoux and the Col du Tourmalet, where his aggressive racing style left his competitors in the dust. His rivalry with Jan Ullrich, the 1997 Tour winner, became a focal point of the races, with Armstrong often gaining psychological and physical advantages over the German cyclist.

In 2001, Armstrong's victory was highlighted by his performance in the Alpe d'Huez, one of the most iconic climbs in the Tour de France. His relentless pace and strategic attacks on the mountain stages cemented his dominance. The infamous 'Look' incident, where Armstrong glanced back at Ullrich before launching a devastating attack, became one of the most memorable moments in Tour history, symbolising his confidence and tactical acumen.

The 2002 and 2003 Tours continued Armstrong's streak of victories. His preparation for these races involved high-altitude training camps, time trial practice, and detailed reconnaissance of key stages. Armstrong's team, now sponsored by U.S. Postal Service, was instrumental in his success. Riders like George Hincapie, Floyd Landis, and Tyler Hamilton provided crucial support, setting a fast pace, protecting Armstrong from the wind, and assisting him in the mountains. The team's strategy was to control the race, setting a tempo that discouraged attacks and kept Armstrong in a favourable position.

In 2004, Armstrong faced increased competition from rising stars like Ivan Basso and Andreas Klöden. Despite the challenges, Armstrong's experience and tactical intelligence saw him prevail once again. His performance in the individual time trials and the mountain stages demonstrated his versatility and endurance. The Col de la Croix de Fer and the climb to La Mongie were scenes of his relentless pursuit of victory, showcasing his ability to suffer and push through pain.

The 2005 Tour de France was Armstrong's final race before his first retirement. It was a testament to his career's consistency and dominance. The race began with a prologue in Fromentine, where Armstrong donned the yellow jersey early on. His team, now known as Discovery Channel, continued their formidable support, ensuring Armstrong remained protected and well-positioned throughout the race. His performance on the Col de la Madeleine and the climb to Courchevel were masterclasses in mountain racing, where his tactical nous and physical strength were unmatched.

Armstrong's seven consecutive Tour de France victories were seen as a remarkable achievement, elevating him to the status of a global sports icon. His story of overcoming cancer and returning to the pinnacle of his sport inspired millions. He became a symbol of resilience, determination, and the triumph of the human spirit. His foundation,

Livestrong, raised millions for cancer research and support, further solidifying his legacy.

However, beneath the surface of Armstrong's success lay a darker reality. Rumours and allegations of doping had followed him throughout his career. Armstrong vehemently denied these claims, often portraying himself as a victim of unfounded accusations. He aggressively defended his reputation, suing those who publicly accused him and maintaining his innocence.

The turning point came in 2010 when Floyd Landis, a former teammate, publicly admitted to doping and implicated Armstrong in a systematic doping programme within the U.S. Postal Service team. This revelation sparked a federal investigation, followed by a comprehensive inquiry by the United States Anti-Doping Agency (USADA). In 2012, USADA released a detailed report outlining widespread doping practices in Armstrong's teams, supported by testimonies from numerous former teammates and associates.

The evidence was overwhelming. Armstrong's use of performance-enhancing drugs, including EPO, blood transfusions, and testosterone, was systematically organised and meticulously concealed. The report detailed how team doctors, managers, and riders were involved in the doping programme, which operated with a high level of sophistication and deception. The findings led to Armstrong being stripped of his seven Tour de France titles and receiving a lifetime ban from professional cycling.

Armstrong's fall from grace was swift and dramatic. In a public interview with Oprah Winfrey in 2013, he admitted to doping throughout his career. The admission shocked the sporting world and disappointed millions of fans who had admired him as a symbol of perseverance and integrity. The impact of the revelations was profound, tarnishing his legacy and raising questions about the culture of professional cycling.

The legacy of Lance Armstrong is complex. On one hand, his achievements in the Tour de France demonstrated remarkable physical and mental prowess. His ability to recover from cancer and return to the top of his sport remains an extraordinary testament to human resilience. However, his use of performance-enhancing drugs and the subsequent deception cast a long shadow over his accomplishments. Armstrong's story is a cautionary tale about the pressures and temptations in elite sports and the consequences of compromising integrity for success.

Armstrong's impact on cycling and sports in general cannot be understated. His rise and fall brought unprecedented attention to the issue of doping, leading to significant reforms in testing and enforcement. The cycling community has since made strides towards greater transparency and accountability, striving to rebuild the sport's credibility.

In the years following his admission, Armstrong has attempted to rebuild his life and reputation. He has been involved in various ventures, including media projects and public speaking, sharing his experiences and lessons learned. While his reputation remains tarnished, his story continues to be a subject of fascination and debate, reflecting the complexities of human nature and the high stakes of competitive sports.

Lance Armstrong's seven Tour de France wins were a remarkable chapter in the history of cycling, characterised by extraordinary athleticism and strategic brilliance. Yet, they were also marked by deception and ethical breaches that ultimately overshadowed his achievements. Armstrong's journey from triumph to disgrace serves as a powerful reminder of the importance of integrity and the enduring impact of one's choices on their legacy.

The Boston Marathon Bombing and Its Aftermath (2013)

The Boston Marathon Bombing on April 15, 2013, remains one of the most harrowing events in recent American history, a day that started with celebration and ended in tragedy. The marathon, held annually on Patriots' Day, is a cherished event, drawing participants and spectators from around the world. The 2013 race was no different, with around 27,000 runners and hundreds of thousands of spectators lining the streets of Boston to cheer them on.

The atmosphere was festive as the marathon unfolded. Families and friends gathered at the finish line on Boylston Street, an area renowned for its vibrant energy and celebratory spirit on race day. Runners, having trained for months, approached the finish line with a mix of exhaustion and exhilaration. The weather was nearly perfect, contributing to the joyful mood. Yet, amidst this jubilation, two brothers, Tamerlan and Dzhokhar Tsarnaev, were preparing to execute a plan that would shatter the peace and security of the event.

The Tsarnaev brothers, originally from Kyrgyzstan, had lived in the United States for about a decade. Tamerlan, the elder brother, had been involved in various controversies, including a failed boxing career and radicalisation influenced by extremist Islamist ideology. Dzhokhar, the younger sibling, was a student at the University of Massachusetts Dartmouth, where he seemed well-integrated and sociable. However, beneath this facade, he shared his brother's radical beliefs.

On the morning of the marathon, the Tsarnaevs placed two homemade bombs near the finish line, concealed in backpacks. These devices were constructed from pressure cookers filled with nails, ball bearings, and other shrapnel, designed to cause maximum injury. As the marathon proceeded, the brothers mingled with the crowd, waiting for the right moment to detonate their deadly devices.

At 2:49 PM, the first bomb exploded near the finish line, followed by a second explosion just 12 seconds later, about 210 yards away. The blasts sent shockwaves through the crowd, creating chaos and panic. Runners stumbled and fell, while spectators, many of whom had come to support loved ones, were thrown to the ground by the force of the explosions. The air filled with smoke, screams, and the blare of emergency sirens.

The immediate aftermath was a scene of devastation. Three people were killed: eight-year-old Martin Richard, 23-year-old Lu Lingzi, a Chinese graduate student at Boston University, and 29-year-old Krystle Campbell, a restaurant manager from nearby Medford. Over 260 others were injured, many suffering severe injuries, including traumatic amputations. First responders and bystanders alike sprang into action, providing aid and comfort amidst the chaos. Medical tents set up for marathon runners were transformed into makeshift triage units, where emergency personnel worked tirelessly to stabilise the wounded before transporting them to nearby hospitals.

The response from law enforcement was swift and extensive. Local, state, and federal agencies coordinated their efforts to secure the area, investigate the crime scene, and launch a manhunt for the perpetrators. The FBI took the lead, labelling the incident as an act of terrorism. Within hours, surveillance footage from nearby businesses and media broadcasts revealed images of the Tsarnaev brothers, identified as the primary suspects.

As the investigation unfolded, the Tsarnaevs attempted to flee. On the evening of April 18, they ambushed and killed MIT police officer Sean Collier in a failed attempt to steal his service weapon. Later that night, the brothers carjacked a vehicle, taking its owner hostage before releasing him unharmed. A dramatic chase ensued, culminating in a violent confrontation with police in Watertown, a suburb of Boston. During the shootout, Tamerlan was critically injured and subsequently run over by his brother as Dzhokhar fled the scene.

The ensuing manhunt for Dzhokhar Tsarnaev paralysed the Boston area. Residents were urged to stay indoors, public transport was suspended, and businesses closed as law enforcement conducted an exhaustive search. The sense of fear and uncertainty was palpable as the city remained in lockdown. On the evening of April 19, a Watertown resident discovered Dzhokhar hiding in a boat stored in his backyard. After a tense standoff, during which Dzhokhar was injured, he was apprehended by law enforcement.

In the days following the bombing, Boston and the wider community began the arduous process of healing and recovery. Hospitals worked tirelessly to treat the injured, many of whom faced long roads to recovery and rehabilitation. Support poured in from across the country and around the world, as people offered donations, words of encouragement, and acts of kindness. The phrase "Boston Strong" emerged as a rallying cry, symbolising the city's resilience and unity in the face of tragedy.

The legal proceedings against Dzhokhar Tsarnaev were highly publicised. Charged with 30 federal counts, including using a weapon of mass destruction and the murder of a police officer, Tsarnaev faced the death penalty. During the trial, the prosecution presented overwhelming evidence of his involvement in the bombing and subsequent crimes, while the defence argued that Tamerlan had been the mastermind, with Dzhokhar acting under his brother's influence. Despite these arguments, the jury found Tsarnaev guilty on all counts, and he was sentenced to death in 2015. The case has since gone through various appeals, reflecting the complexities and ongoing debates surrounding the death penalty in the United States.

The Boston Marathon Bombing had far-reaching effects on security protocols for public events. Authorities across the country re-evaluated and enhanced their security measures to prevent similar attacks. Major sporting events, concerts, and public gatherings saw increased police presence, surveillance, and stricter regulations regarding bags and personal items. The lessons learned from Boston have been instrumental in shaping how large-scale events are secured, aiming to balance safety with the public's ability to enjoy these events.

The psychological impact of the bombing on survivors and the community was profound. Many of those who were injured, as well as their families, struggled with post-traumatic stress disorder, anxiety, and depression. Support groups, counselling services, and community initiatives played a crucial role in helping individuals cope with the aftermath. The sense of solidarity and mutual support that emerged in the wake of the bombing highlighted the strength of the human spirit and the importance of community in the healing process.

In the years following the bombing, the Boston Marathon has continued to be a symbol of resilience and defiance. The event has grown in significance, with increased participation and spectatorship. Each year, the marathon honours the memory of those who lost their lives and celebrates the strength of the survivors. The presence of those who were injured, many of whom have returned to complete the race, serves as a powerful testament to the human capacity for recovery and determination.

The Boston Marathon Bombing also highlighted the critical role of first responders and medical professionals. The quick and effective actions of police, firefighters, paramedics, and medical staff saved countless lives and mitigated the impact of the injuries sustained. Their dedication and bravery were widely recognised, and the event underscored the importance of preparedness and training for emergency situations.

The community's response to the bombing demonstrated the power of collective action in times of crisis. Fundraisers, charity events, and memorials were organised to support the victims and their families. The One Fund Boston, established by Governor Deval Patrick and Mayor Thomas Menino, raised over $80 million to assist those affected by the bombing. This outpouring of generosity and compassion reflected the deep sense of solidarity and the desire to help those in need.

In the broader context, the Boston Marathon Bombing served as a stark reminder of the ongoing threat of terrorism and the challenges associated with preventing and responding to such attacks. It prompted a re-evaluation of intelligence and counter-terrorism strategies, emphasising the need for vigilance, coordination, and international cooperation. The incident also sparked discussions about radicalisation, the influence of extremist ideologies, and the importance of addressing the root causes of terrorism.

The cultural impact of the bombing has been significant, with numerous books, documentaries, and films exploring the events and their aftermath. These works have helped to keep the memory of the victims alive, educate the public about the incident, and provide insights into the experiences of those directly affected. They also serve as a testament to the resilience and courage of the survivors, first responders, and the Boston community.

The legacy of the Boston Marathon Bombing is multifaceted, encompassing themes of tragedy, resilience, and recovery. It stands as a powerful example of how communities can come together in the face of adversity, support one another, and emerge stronger. The stories of those who lost their lives, those who survived, and those who responded to the crisis are a testament to the enduring human spirit and the capacity for compassion and solidarity.

As the years pass, the Boston Marathon continues to be a symbol of strength and perseverance. The event has taken on new meaning, serving as a reminder of the challenges faced and the progress made in the wake of the bombing. The collective memory of that fateful day, the bravery displayed, and the unity that emerged in its aftermath will forever be a part of the marathon's history and the city's identity.

In reflecting on the Boston Marathon Bombing, it is important to honour the memory of the victims, support the ongoing recovery of the survivors, and recognise the contributions of those who responded to the crisis. The lessons learned from this tragic event continue to inform efforts to prevent and respond to acts of terrorism, ensuring that the legacy of resilience and strength endures. The story of the Boston

Marathon Bombing is one of loss and sorrow, but also of hope, courage, and the unwavering human spirit.

Diego Maradona's "Hand of God" (1986 World Cup)

Diego Maradona's "Hand of God" and "Goal of the Century" in the 1986 World Cup are among the most famous and controversial moments in the history of football. The Argentine maestro, known for his extraordinary skill and controversial personality, crafted these unforgettable moments during the quarter-final match between Argentina and England on June 22, 1986, at the Estadio Azteca in Mexico City. The backdrop of the match was charged with historical and political tension, given the Falklands War between Argentina and the United Kingdom just four years earlier. Against this backdrop, Maradona's actions would cement his legacy both as a footballing genius and a controversial figure.

Diego Maradona was born in Villa Fiorito, a shantytown on the outskirts of Buenos Aires, Argentina, in 1960. From a young age, it was clear that Maradona possessed a unique talent. His incredible dribbling skills, vision, and flair set him apart from his peers. He joined Argentinos Juniors as a youth player and made his professional debut at the age of 15. His performances quickly attracted attention, and he moved to Boca Juniors, one of Argentina's most prestigious clubs. Success at Boca Juniors led to a move to Europe, where Maradona joined FC Barcelona before moving to Napoli in Italy. At Napoli, Maradona became a legend, leading the club to unprecedented success. Despite his club achievements, the World Cup remained the ultimate stage for Maradona to showcase his abilities.

The 1986 World Cup in Mexico provided Maradona with the perfect platform to shine. Argentina, managed by Carlos Bilardo, was a team built around Maradona's talents. Bilardo's tactical approach allowed Maradona the freedom to roam and create, while the rest of the team provided a solid foundation. Maradona arrived at the tournament in peak form, determined to lead his country to glory. Argentina progressed through the group stage and the knockout rounds, setting up a quarter-final clash with England. The match was highly anticipated, not just for the footballing rivalry but also due to the recent conflict between the two nations.

As the match began, it was clear that Maradona was in scintillating form. The first half was a tense and closely fought affair, with both teams having chances but neither able to break the deadlock. The match reached its turning point in the 51st minute. Maradona received the ball outside the England penalty area and began a darting run towards the goal. As he reached the edge of the box, he attempted a one-two with Jorge Valdano, but the ball was deflected by England's Steve Hodge, looping into the air towards the goal. Maradona continued his run and, seeing the ball dropping near the goal, leapt to challenge England goalkeeper Peter Shilton. Using his left hand, Maradona punched the ball into the net. The referee, Ali Bin Nasser, did not see the handball and allowed the goal to stand despite the protests from the England players. Maradona later described the goal as "a little with the head of Maradona and a little with the hand of God," coining the now-famous term "Hand of God."

Just four minutes after this controversial goal, Maradona delivered what is widely regarded as the greatest goal in World Cup history. Picking up the ball in his own half, he embarked on a solo run that would become legendary. He dribbled past five England players, weaving his way through the midfield and defence with sublime skill and balance. Maradona's pace, control, and agility were on full display as he left the England players trailing in his wake. As he entered the penalty area, he feinted past Terry Butcher and Peter Shilton before calmly slotting the ball into the net. The entire sequence took just ten seconds and covered over 60 yards. The goal was a masterpiece, a moment of pure footballing brilliance that would forever be known as the "Goal of the Century."

England managed to pull a goal back through Gary Lineker, but Argentina held on to win the match 2-1. Maradona's performance was the defining factor in the victory, his two contrasting goals encapsulating both the controversy and genius of his play. The "Hand of God" was a moment of audacity and deception, while the "Goal of the Century" was a demonstration of his extraordinary talent and flair. The match solidified Maradona's status as a footballing icon and a national hero in Argentina.

Following the quarter-final, Argentina advanced to the semi-finals, where they faced Belgium. Maradona once again took centre stage, scoring both goals in a 2-0 victory to propel Argentina into the final. In the final, Argentina faced West Germany. The match was a thrilling contest, with Argentina taking a 2-0 lead before West Germany fought back to level the score at 2-2. Maradona, tightly marked throughout the match, still managed to make a decisive impact. In the 86th minute, he delivered a perfectly weighted pass to Jorge Burruchaga, who scored the winning goal. Argentina triumphed 3-2, and Maradona lifted the World Cup trophy, achieving his dream of leading his country to glory.

The 1986 World Cup was Maradona's tournament. He was awarded the Golden Ball as the best player, having scored five goals and provided five assists. His performances were a showcase of his unique talent, vision, and ability to influence matches. Maradona's achievements in Mexico cemented his place among the greatest footballers of all time.

Maradona's career following the 1986 World Cup was marked by further successes and controversies. He continued to excel at Napoli, leading the club to two Serie A titles and a UEFA Cup victory. However, his career was also plagued by issues off the pitch, including struggles with addiction and disciplinary problems. Despite these challenges, Maradona's impact on the game remained undiminished. He was revered in Argentina and adored by Napoli fans, who saw him as a saviour who brought unprecedented success to their club.

The "Hand of God" and "Goal of the Century" remain indelible moments in the history of football. They are emblematic of Maradona's complex legacy, showcasing both his genius and his willingness to bend the rules. The "Hand of God" continues to be a topic of debate and discussion, often cited as one of the most infamous moments in the sport. In contrast, the "Goal of the Century" is universally celebrated as a moment of pure brilliance, a testament to Maradona's unparalleled skill and creativity.

Maradona's legacy extends beyond his achievements on the pitch. He is remembered as a cultural icon, a figure who transcended football and became a symbol of hope and inspiration for millions. His rise from the slums of Villa Fiorito to the pinnacle of world football is a story of determination, resilience, and extraordinary talent. Maradona's influence on the game is evident in the countless players who have been inspired by his style and flair.

The impact of Maradona's performances in the 1986 World Cup is still felt today. His goals against England are replayed and celebrated, serving as reminders of his remarkable ability and the drama of the sport. The "Hand of God" and "Goal of the Century" are part of football's rich tapestry, moments that capture the essence of the game and the magic it can produce.

In Argentina, Maradona is a national hero, revered for his contributions to the country's footballing history. His achievements in the 1986 World Cup are a source of immense pride and a symbol of Argentina's footballing prowess. Maradona's influence on Argentine football is profound, with generations of players idolising him and aspiring to emulate his success.

Diego Maradona passed away in 2020, but his legacy lives on. His performances in the 1986 World Cup, particularly the "Hand of God" and "Goal of the Century," remain among the most iconic moments in the history of the sport. Maradona's story is one of triumph and adversity, genius and controversy, encapsulating the beauty and complexity of football. His name will forever be associated with the magic and drama of the game, a reminder of the heights that can be achieved through talent, determination, and a touch of audacity.

The 2008 Wimbledon Final - Federer vs. Nadal

The 2008 Wimbledon Final between Roger Federer and Rafael Nadal is widely regarded as one of the greatest tennis matches in history. The match, which took place on July 6, 2008, at the All England Club in London, was a dramatic and thrilling encounter that showcased the talents and determination of two of the sport's greatest players. This epic battle not only defined a rivalry but also etched their names in the annals of tennis history.

Roger Federer, born in Basel, Switzerland, had established himself as one of the most dominant players in the history of tennis. By 2008, Federer had already secured five consecutive Wimbledon titles, cementing his reputation as the king of grass courts. His style of play, characterised by a graceful blend of powerful serves, precise volleys, and an elegant one-handed backhand, made him a formidable opponent on any surface. Federer's dominance was further evidenced by his record number of Grand Slam titles and his status as the world number one.

Rafael Nadal, hailing from Mallorca, Spain, was the rising star poised to challenge Federer's supremacy. Known for his relentless work ethic, fierce competitive spirit, and an exceptional level of athleticism, Nadal had become the undisputed king of clay courts, winning multiple French Open titles. His game was built on incredible speed, powerful topspin forehands, and a tenacious fighting spirit. Nadal's emergence as a major contender on grass courts added a new dimension to his rivalry with Federer.

The 2008 season had already seen several memorable encounters between Federer and Nadal. Their rivalry was intense and well-documented, with Nadal often getting the better of Federer on clay, while Federer dominated on grass. As the Wimbledon Championships approached, anticipation for a possible final showdown between these two giants of the game reached fever pitch.

The All England Club, with its storied history and immaculate grass courts, provided the perfect setting for this historic clash. Wimbledon, the oldest and most prestigious tennis tournament in the world, is renowned for its traditions and elegance. The Centre Court, where the final would be played, is the epicentre of this grandeur, with its lush green grass and a capacity crowd of nearly 15,000 spectators. The atmosphere on that July day was electric, with fans eagerly awaiting the showdown between Federer and Nadal.

Federer, the defending champion, entered the final seeking his sixth consecutive Wimbledon title, a feat that would further solidify his legacy. Nadal, on the other hand, was determined to win his first Wimbledon title and prove that he could challenge Federer's dominance on grass. Both players had navigated the earlier rounds with relative ease, setting the stage for an epic confrontation.

The match began with Nadal serving, and he quickly established his presence with powerful groundstrokes and aggressive play. Nadal's relentless energy and determination were evident from the start, as he broke Federer's serve early in the first set. Federer's usually unflappable demeanour showed signs of strain as he struggled to find his rhythm against Nadal's relentless assault. Nadal's dominance continued, and he took the first set 6-4, sending a clear message that he was ready to dethrone the champion.

The second set followed a similar pattern, with Nadal maintaining his aggressive play and Federer struggling to counter. Nadal's forehand, one of the most potent weapons in tennis, was firing on all cylinders, and he broke Federer's serve once again to take a commanding lead. Despite Federer's efforts to mount a comeback, Nadal held firm and clinched the second set 6-4. With a two-set lead, Nadal was on the brink of achieving a historic victory.

Federer, known for his resilience and ability to rise to the occasion, faced a daunting challenge. Losing two sets to love in a Wimbledon final was uncharted territory for him. However, the Swiss maestro dug deep, drawing on his vast experience and fighting spirit. The third set saw Federer elevate his game, showcasing the brilliance that had made him a five-time champion. His serve improved, and his groundstrokes became more precise. The set progressed to a tiebreak, where Federer demonstrated his mental toughness and skill, winning it 7-6 to keep his hopes alive.

The fourth set was a testament to the incredible level of tennis both players were producing. The intensity and quality of play reached new heights, with each point being fiercely contested. Federer's serve, a crucial aspect of his game, remained strong, while Nadal continued to push his opponent with relentless pressure. The set once again reached a tiebreak, and Federer, showing incredible composure, edged out Nadal 7-6 to level the match at two sets apiece.

As the match entered the fifth set, the tension and excitement were palpable. The players had already been on court for several hours, and their physical and mental endurance was being tested to the limit. The final set saw both Federer and Nadal produce some of their best tennis, with each game becoming a battle of wills. Rain interruptions added to the drama, forcing the players to regroup and maintain their focus during the breaks.

With the score tied at 7-7 in the final set, Nadal managed to break Federer's serve, gaining a crucial advantage. Serving for the championship at 8-7, Nadal faced immense pressure, but his determination and resilience shone through. After a gruelling rally, Nadal hit a powerful forehand that Federer could only return into the net. With that, Nadal fell to the ground in jubilation, having won the final set 9-7 and secured his first Wimbledon title.

The match, which lasted nearly five hours, was an extraordinary display of skill, athleticism, and mental fortitude. Nadal's victory was a testament to his relentless work ethic and unwavering belief in his abilities. He had dethroned the five-time champion in one of the greatest matches ever played, marking a significant moment in his career.

For Federer, the loss was a bitter disappointment, but his performance in the match underscored his status as one of the greatest players of all time. Despite falling short, his ability to fight back from two sets down and push Nadal to the limit was a remarkable achievement. Federer's grace in defeat further endeared him to fans around the world, who admired his sportsmanship and dedication.

The 2008 Wimbledon Final between Federer and Nadal remains an iconic moment in the history of tennis. It showcased the best of the sport, with two of its greatest players producing a match of unparalleled quality and drama. The encounter not only defined their rivalry but also left an indelible mark on the sport, inspiring future generations of players and fans alike. The legacy of that match continues to resonate, a reminder of the beauty and intensity of tennis at its highest level.

Tiger Woods' 1997 Masters Victory

Tiger Woods' 1997 Masters victory stands as one of the most significant moments in golf history, representing not just a triumph for Woods himself but a transformative event for the sport. Eldrick Tont "Tiger" Woods, born in Cypress, California, on December 30, 1975, was a prodigious talent from a young age. His father, Earl Woods, a former Green Beret and an amateur golfer, introduced him to the game when he was just a toddler. Earl saw immense potential in his son, nurturing his skills with a rigorous training regimen that emphasised both physical ability and mental toughness.

Woods' rise through the ranks of amateur golf was meteoric. By the age of 15, he had already won multiple Junior World Golf Championships. His success continued through his teenage years, culminating in three consecutive U.S. Amateur titles from 1994 to 1996. These victories not only showcased his prodigious talent but also his ability to perform under pressure, traits that would define his professional career.

Turning professional in 1996, Woods immediately made an impact. His first PGA Tour victory came at the Las Vegas Invitational, followed by another win at the Walt Disney World/Oldsmobile Classic. These early successes, combined with his charismatic personality and the marketing prowess of Nike, who had signed him to a lucrative endorsement deal, quickly made Woods a household name. However, it was his performance at the 1997 Masters that would catapult him to global superstardom.

The Masters, held annually at Augusta National Golf Club in Augusta, Georgia, is one of golf's most prestigious tournaments. Augusta National, with its perfectly manicured fairways, fast greens, and iconic holes such as Amen Corner, represents the pinnacle of golfing excellence. The course's history, traditions, and exclusivity add to its mystique, making a victory at the Masters a defining achievement for any golfer.

Heading into the 1997 Masters, Woods was already considered a potential contender, despite it being his first appearance as a professional. His combination of power, precision, and mental fortitude set him apart from his peers. The opening round, however, did not go as planned. Woods struggled on the front nine, making the turn at four-over-par 40, a score that would usually signal a tough road ahead. Yet, the back nine saw a remarkable transformation. Woods found his rhythm, birdieing five of the final seven holes to finish with a two-under-par 70, putting him in contention.

The second round was where Woods began to separate himself from the field. With a dazzling display of power and precision, he shot a record-tying 66, moving to the top of the leaderboard. His driving distance was extraordinary, often leaving himself short irons into greens where others were hitting long irons or woods. Augusta National, traditionally a course that required strategic positioning, was being overpowered by Woods' length off the tee.

By the end of the third round, Woods had built a commanding lead. His 65 on Saturday left him 15-under-par for the tournament, nine strokes clear of his nearest competitor. This performance included memorable shots such as the eagle on the par-five 13th, where he hit a majestic second shot to within a few feet of the hole. The gallery at Augusta National was in awe, witnessing what appeared to be the coronation of a new king in golf.

The final round of the 1997 Masters was less about whether Woods would win and more about by how much. Maintaining his composure and focus, Woods played a solid round, avoiding any major mistakes and continuing to showcase his incredible talent. His final score of 18-under-par 270 set a new Masters record, breaking the previous mark held by Jack Nicklaus and Raymond Floyd. Woods' victory margin of 12 strokes was the largest in Masters history, surpassing Nicklaus' nine-stroke win in 1965.

Woods' victory at the 1997 Masters was significant for several reasons. It marked the arrival of a new era in golf, dominated by his unique blend of power, precision, and mental toughness. His performance at Augusta National shattered records and redefined what was possible in the game. Moreover, Woods' win had a profound cultural impact. As the first African American to win the Masters, Woods broke down racial barriers in a sport that had long been perceived as exclusive and predominantly white. His victory inspired a new generation of golfers from diverse backgrounds, broadening the appeal of the game globally.

Woods' dominance at the 1997 Masters was not just a result of his physical abilities but also his mental approach. Throughout the tournament, he displayed an unshakeable focus, maintaining his composure even under the intense pressure of leading a major championship. His ability to block out distractions and execute shots with precision was a testament to the mental training instilled by his father from a young age. Earl Woods had taught Tiger to remain calm and composed, using techniques such as visualisation and meditation to enhance his concentration and resilience.

The 1997 Masters also highlighted Woods' strategic acumen. While his driving distance garnered much attention, it was his course management and decision-making that set him apart. Woods understood the nuances of Augusta National, knowing when to attack and when to play conservatively. His ability to read the greens and judge the speed and break of his putts was exceptional, leading to several crucial birdies and par saves throughout the tournament. This combination of power, precision, and strategy made Woods a formidable competitor and a true master of the game.

Woods' victory at the Masters had a ripple effect across the golfing world. Equipment manufacturers began to innovate, producing clubs and balls designed to maximise distance and control, catering to the new standard set by Woods. Golf courses, too, underwent changes, with many lengthening their layouts and redesigning holes to present a greater challenge to the modern golfer. Woods' influence on the game was profound, ushering in an era of technological advancement and athleticism that continues to shape the sport today.

The impact of Woods' win extended beyond the confines of golf. His victory resonated with people around the world, transcending the sport and becoming a cultural phenomenon. Woods' success inspired countless individuals, particularly those from underrepresented communities, to take up golf and pursue their dreams. His story of perseverance, talent, and triumph served as a beacon of hope and possibility, demonstrating that barriers could be broken and new heights achieved.

In the years following his 1997 Masters victory, Woods continued to dominate the world of golf. He amassed numerous major championships, setting records and solidifying his status as one of the greatest golfers of all time. His influence extended to charitable work, with the establishment of the Tiger Woods Foundation, which aimed to provide educational opportunities and support for underserved youth. Woods' legacy in golf and beyond is a testament to his enduring impact on the sport and society.

The 1997 Masters victory remains a defining moment in Woods' career and in the history of golf. It marked the beginning of an era of unprecedented dominance and innovation, with Woods leading the charge. His performance at Augusta National showcased the pinnacle of golfing excellence, combining physical prowess, mental fortitude, and strategic brilliance. Woods' win not only changed the course of his career but also transformed the sport, inspiring a new generation of golfers and leaving an indelible mark on the game.

The legacy of Tiger Woods' 1997 Masters victory endures to this day. It is remembered as a moment of extraordinary achievement, where talent, hard work, and determination converged to create history. Woods' triumph at Augusta National remains an iconic chapter in the annals of golf, symbolising the limitless potential of human endeavour and the enduring spirit of the game. As future generations look back on this historic victory, they will continue to draw inspiration from Woods' remarkable journey and the indomitable will that propelled him to greatness.

Babe Ruth's Called Shot (1932 World Series)

Babe Ruth's "Called Shot" during the 1932 World Series is one of the most enduring legends in baseball history. This iconic moment, occurring in Game 3 between the New York Yankees and the Chicago Cubs at Wrigley Field, has been immortalised in sports lore, symbolising the larger-than-life persona of Ruth and the mystique of baseball. To understand the significance of this moment, it's important to delve into the character of Babe Ruth, the setting of the event, the build-up to the 1932 World Series, and the dramatic context in which this legendary act unfolded.

George Herman "Babe" Ruth, born in Baltimore, Maryland, in 1895, transformed the landscape of baseball with his prodigious talent and charismatic presence. Known for his towering home runs and flamboyant lifestyle, Ruth was a figure who transcended the sport. He began his career as a pitcher for the Boston Red Sox but later became famous as a slugging outfielder for the New York Yankees. By 1932, Ruth was nearing the end of his illustrious career but remained a formidable force in the Yankees' lineup.

Wrigley Field, the venerable ballpark of the Chicago Cubs, was the setting for Game 3 of the 1932 World Series. Known for its ivy-covered walls and intimate atmosphere, Wrigley Field was a fitting stage for what would become one of baseball's most memorable moments. The Cubs, a storied franchise with a passionate fan base, were eager to challenge the Yankees' dominance. The 1932 season had seen both teams perform strongly, with the Yankees winning the American League pennant and the Cubs securing the National League title.

The lead-up to the World Series was marked by tension and rivalry. The Yankees, managed by Joe McCarthy, were a powerhouse team featuring stars like Lou Gehrig, Tony Lazzeri, and Bill Dickey alongside Ruth. Their formidable lineup was matched by a strong pitching staff, making them the favourites to win the series. The Cubs, under manager Charlie Grimm, were determined to upset the Yankees. Their roster included standout players like Hack Wilson, Billy Herman, and Gabby Hartnett, who were capable of turning the tide in any game.

The first two games of the series, held at Yankee Stadium, saw the Yankees take a commanding 2-0 lead. Ruth played a pivotal role, showcasing his batting prowess and setting the stage for the dramatic events to come. The series then moved to Chicago, where the Cubs hoped to use their home-field advantage to mount a comeback.

Game 3, played on October 1, 1932, was a pivotal contest. The atmosphere at Wrigley Field was electric, with a capacity crowd eagerly anticipating the clash. The game began with the Yankees taking an early lead, but the Cubs quickly responded, keeping the contest close. The tension on the field mirrored the intensity in the stands, where Cubs fans jeered Ruth and his teammates. The back-and-forth nature of the game added to the drama, as both teams fought to gain the upper hand.

The moment that would become legend occurred in the fifth inning. With the score tied at 4-4, Ruth stepped to the plate to face Cubs pitcher Charlie Root. The animosity between the two teams was palpable, and the crowd's taunts reached a fever pitch. As Ruth settled into the batter's box, he engaged in a heated exchange with the Cubs' dugout and the fans. Accounts of what happened next vary, but the most famous version is that Ruth pointed towards the centre-field bleachers, seemingly indicating where he intended to hit the next pitch.

Root delivered a fastball, and Ruth swung with his characteristic power. The ball soared high and deep, heading straight towards the centre-field stands. As it cleared the fence, the crowd erupted, some in disbelief and others in awe. Ruth had delivered on his audacious gesture, hitting a home run that would forever be known as the "Called Shot." The Yankees took the lead, and Ruth's home run became the defining moment of the game. The Yankees went on to win the game and ultimately swept the Cubs to claim the World Series title.

The "Called Shot" was more than just a home run; it was a moment that encapsulated the essence of Babe Ruth. His bravado, skill, and larger-than-life personality combined to create a lasting image that has been debated and celebrated for decades. Whether or not Ruth actually pointed to the stands with the intention of calling his shot remains a matter of historical conjecture, but the impact of the event is undeniable.

In the aftermath of the game, accounts of Ruth's gesture varied. Some players and spectators insisted that Ruth had indeed called his shot, pointing to the stands before launching the home run. Others, including Root, dismissed the notion as a myth, suggesting that Ruth was merely responding to the taunts from the Cubs' dugout. Despite the differing perspectives, the legend of the "Called Shot" grew, fuelled by Ruth's own retellings and the media's fascination with the story.

Ruth's performance in the 1932 World Series was emblematic of his career. He finished the series with a .333 batting average, two home runs, and six RBIs, demonstrating his ability to deliver in crucial moments. The Yankees' victory added to their legacy as one of the most successful franchises in baseball history, and Ruth's contributions were central to their triumph.

The legacy of the "Called Shot" extends beyond the confines of the 1932 World Series. It has become a symbol of Ruth's impact on the game and his enduring influence on baseball culture. Ruth's ability to captivate audiences with his prodigious talent and larger-than-life persona helped to elevate the sport's popularity and cement his status as a cultural icon. The story of the "Called Shot" has been passed down through generations, inspiring countless fans and players alike.

In the years following the 1932 World Series, Ruth's career began to wind down. He played his final seasons with the Yankees before a brief stint with the Boston Braves. Despite the decline in his on-field performance, Ruth's legacy continued to grow. He retired in 1935 with 714 career home runs, a record that would stand for nearly four decades. His impact on the game extended beyond his statistical achievements; Ruth helped to popularise baseball and transform it into America's pastime.

The "Called Shot" remains a testament to Ruth's unique blend of talent and showmanship. It exemplifies his ability to perform under pressure and his flair for the dramatic. The event has been immortalised in various forms, from books and documentaries to statues and museum exhibits. The image of Ruth pointing to the stands, whether factual or embellished, captures the imagination and evokes the spirit of an era when baseball was defined by larger-than-life figures and unforgettable moments.

Ruth's legacy continues to be celebrated in the world of baseball. His influence can be seen in the way the game is played, marketed, and appreciated. Modern players who display power and charisma are often compared to Ruth, highlighting his lasting impact on the sport. The "Called Shot" is a defining chapter in the story of Babe Ruth, a moment that encapsulates his greatness and the magic of baseball.

In examining the broader context of the "Called Shot," it is important to recognise the cultural and historical significance of the event. Ruth's career unfolded during a time of great change in America, as the country grappled with economic challenges and social transformations. Baseball, as a national pastime, provided a sense of continuity and escape for many Americans. Ruth's exploits on the field, including the "Called Shot," offered moments of joy and inspiration during an era marked by uncertainty.

The 1932 World Series, and specifically the "Called Shot," also highlights the role of narrative and myth-making in sports. The stories we tell about athletes and their achievements help to shape our understanding of the game and its heroes. Ruth's "Called Shot" is a prime example of how a single moment can be elevated to legendary status, becoming part of the collective memory and identity of a sport.

The enduring appeal of the "Called Shot" lies in its blend of fact and folklore. While the exact details of Ruth's gesture may be debated, the essence of the story captures the imagination and embodies the spirit of competition and showmanship. It is a reminder that sports are not just about statistics and outcomes, but also about the moments that transcend the game and resonate with fans on a deeper level.

As we reflect on Babe Ruth's "Called Shot," it is clear that this moment represents more than just a home run. It symbolises the power of sports to inspire, entertain, and unite. Ruth's larger-than-life persona and his ability to perform in the most dramatic of circumstances continue to captivate audiences and inspire future generations of athletes. The "Called Shot" is a timeless reminder of the magic and mystery that make baseball, and sports in general, an integral part of our cultural fabric.

Babe Ruth's "Called Shot" during the 1932 World Series is a defining moment in the history of baseball. It encapsulates the essence of Ruth's greatness and the enduring allure of the sport. The event's blend of fact and folklore, combined with Ruth's larger-than-life persona, has ensured its place in the pantheon of baseball legends. The "Called Shot" remains a symbol of the magic and drama that make sports an integral part of our cultural heritage. Ruth's legacy, embodied in this iconic moment, continues to inspire and captivate, reminding us of the enduring power of sports to create unforgettable memories and timeless stories.

Jackie Robinson Breaks the Colour Barrier (1947)

Jackie Robinson's breaking of the colour barrier in Major League Baseball in 1947 stands as a monumental event in both sports and American history. Born in Cairo, Georgia, in 1919, Robinson grew up in a time of profound racial segregation and inequality. His journey to becoming the first African American to play in the Major Leagues was fraught with challenges, but his talent, determination, and the unwavering support of key individuals paved the way for this historic achievement.

Robinson was raised in Pasadena, California, by a single mother after his father abandoned the family. Growing up in a predominantly white neighbourhood, Robinson experienced racism from an early age. Despite these challenges, he excelled in sports, displaying remarkable talent in football, basketball, track, and baseball during his high school and college years. Robinson attended UCLA, where he became the first athlete to letter in four varsity sports. His prowess on the athletic field was matched by his resilience and leadership, qualities that would prove crucial in his later career.

After leaving UCLA, Robinson briefly played semi-professional football before being drafted into the Army during World War II. His military service was marked by an incident in which he refused to move to the back of a segregated bus, leading to a court-martial. Robinson was eventually acquitted, but this experience further solidified his resolve to fight against racial injustice. Following his discharge, he played for the Kansas City Monarchs in the Negro Leagues, where his talent caught the attention of Brooklyn Dodgers general manager Branch Rickey.

Branch Rickey, a visionary and shrewd businessman, was determined to integrate Major League Baseball. Rickey understood that signing an African American player would not only be morally just but also beneficial for the sport and his team. He sought a player with exceptional talent and the fortitude to withstand the inevitable racism and hostility that would come with breaking the colour barrier. Rickey found this in Jackie Robinson.

In 1945, Rickey approached Robinson with the offer to join the Dodgers organisation. Their meeting was intense and emotional, with Rickey emphasising the immense challenges Robinson would face. He needed assurance that Robinson would not respond to the inevitable provocations with violence or anger. Robinson, recognising the significance of this opportunity, promised to restrain his emotions and endure the hardships for the greater cause. With this agreement, Robinson signed with the Dodgers, becoming the first African American to join a Major League team in the modern era.

Robinson's journey to the Major Leagues began with the Montreal Royals, the Dodgers' top minor league team. In 1946, Robinson took the field for the Royals, becoming the first African American to play in the International League. His debut was a resounding success; he led the league in batting average and helped the Royals win the championship. Despite his on-field success, Robinson faced relentless racism from fans, opponents, and even some teammates. He endured racial slurs, threats, and segregation but maintained his composure, demonstrating his exceptional character and resilience.

The stage was set for Robinson to make his Major League debut in 1947. On April 15, he took the field for the Brooklyn Dodgers, playing first base against the Boston Braves at Ebbets Field. The significance of this moment was profound. For the first time in over 50 years, an African American was playing in the Major Leagues. Robinson's presence on the field symbolised a major step towards racial integration in sports and American society.

Robinson's debut season was extraordinary. He faced intense scrutiny and hostility from fans, opponents, and some of his own teammates. Many teams and players threatened to boycott games, and Robinson was subjected to racial slurs and violent threats. Despite this, he maintained his dignity and focused on his performance. Robinson's talent was undeniable; he batted .297, led the league in stolen bases, and was named Rookie of the Year. His contributions helped the Dodgers win the National League pennant, marking a successful season both personally and for the team.

Throughout the 1947 season, Robinson's impact extended beyond his athletic achievements. His presence challenged the entrenched racial segregation in baseball and American society. Robinson's courage and determination inspired other African American athletes and played a crucial role in the broader civil rights movement. His success demonstrated that talent and hard work, not race, should determine one's opportunities and achievements.

One of the key moments in Robinson's rookie season occurred during a game against the Philadelphia Phillies. The Phillies' manager, Ben Chapman, and his players hurled vicious racial insults at Robinson from the dugout. This incident was particularly egregious, highlighting the pervasive racism Robinson faced. However, it also rallied support for him from his teammates and fans. Dodgers captain Pee Wee Reese famously put his arm around Robinson in a show of solidarity during another game, symbolising the growing acceptance and support for Robinson within the team and the sport.

Robinson's integration of Major League Baseball had a ripple effect. Other teams soon followed the Dodgers' lead, signing African American players. Larry Doby became the first African American to play in the American League, joining the Cleveland Indians just a few months after Robinson's debut. Over the next few years, more African American and Latino players entered the Major Leagues, breaking down racial barriers and transforming the sport.

Robinson's impact was not limited to the baseball diamond. He became an outspoken advocate for civil rights, using his platform to challenge racial discrimination and promote equality. He collaborated with prominent civil rights leaders, including Martin Luther King Jr., and participated in various civil rights initiatives. Robinson's influence extended to politics as well; he supported candidates who championed civil rights and spoke out against policies and politicians that perpetuated racial injustice.

Despite the progress that Robinson's career symbolised, he continued to face challenges and adversity. Racism persisted both on and off the field, and Robinson's outspokenness sometimes made him a target. Nevertheless, he remained steadfast in his commitment to equality and justice. His legacy extended beyond his playing career, as he continued to advocate for civil rights and social change until his death in 1972.

Robinson's contributions to baseball and society were recognised and celebrated in numerous ways. He was inducted into the Baseball Hall of Fame in 1962, becoming the first African American to receive this honour. Major League Baseball retired his number, 42, across all teams in 1997, marking the 50th anniversary of his debut. This unprecedented gesture ensured that Robinson's legacy would be remembered and honoured by future generations.

The story of Jackie Robinson breaking the colour barrier in 1947 is a testament to his exceptional talent, courage, and resilience. It highlights the power of sports as a platform for social change and the importance of challenging injustice and inequality. Robinson's journey was not just a personal triumph but a pivotal moment in the broader struggle for civil rights and racial integration in America. His legacy continues to inspire athletes, activists, and individuals committed to promoting equality and justice in all areas of society.

The impact of Robinson's achievements extends to the present day. His story is a reminder of the progress that has been made and the work that remains in the fight for racial equality. Robinson's legacy is celebrated each year on April 15, known as Jackie Robinson Day, when players across Major League Baseball wear his number 42 in tribute. This tradition serves as a reminder of Robinson's contributions and the enduring significance of his breaking the colour barrier.

In addition to his on-field accomplishments, Robinson's influence is evident in the increased diversity within Major League Baseball and other professional sports. The path he paved has allowed countless athletes of colour to pursue their dreams and achieve success at the highest levels. Robinson's story also underscores the importance of allies and advocates who support and stand in solidarity with those facing discrimination and injustice.

The story of Jackie Robinson breaking the colour barrier in 1947 is a powerful example of how individuals can drive social change and challenge the status quo. It highlights the importance of perseverance, courage, and the willingness to stand up for what is right, even in the face of overwhelming adversity. Robinson's legacy serves as an enduring source of inspiration and a reminder of the transformative power of sports and the human spirit.

Jim Thorpe at the 1912 Olympics

Jim Thorpe's performance at the 1912 Olympics is one of the most remarkable and inspiring stories in the history of sports. Born in 1887 near Prague, Oklahoma, Thorpe was of mixed Native American and European ancestry, belonging to the Sac and Fox Nation. His upbringing on the reservation was marked by a connection to his cultural roots and an early demonstration of his extraordinary athletic talents. Thorpe faced many challenges from a young age, including the death of his twin brother and later his mother, which had a profound impact on his life.

Thorpe's athletic prowess began to shine through during his time at the Carlisle Indian Industrial School in Pennsylvania. Carlisle was designed to assimilate Native American children into American society, often stripping them of their cultural identities. Despite the oppressive environment, Thorpe's talent could not be contained. He excelled in multiple sports under the guidance of coach Pop Warner, one of the most influential figures in early American football. Warner recognised Thorpe's unique abilities and encouraged him to pursue various athletic disciplines, leading to his dominance in track and field, football, baseball, and even ballroom dancing.

Leading up to the 1912 Olympics, Thorpe had already made a name for himself in collegiate sports, particularly in track and field and football. His versatility and raw athleticism caught the attention of the American Olympic Committee, which was looking for athletes to compete in the upcoming Games in Stockholm, Sweden. The 1912 Olympics were to be a grand event, showcasing athletes from around the world in a variety of disciplines, including the newly introduced pentathlon and decathlon, events that would test an athlete's overall skill, endurance, and versatility.

Stockholm's Olympic Stadium was a state-of-the-art facility for its time, designed to accommodate a wide range of events and a large number of spectators. The atmosphere was charged with excitement and anticipation, as athletes from different nations prepared to compete at the highest level. Thorpe, representing the United States, was determined to prove himself on this international stage.

Thorpe's journey to Stockholm was not without its challenges. As a Native American, he faced racial discrimination and prejudice both in the United States and abroad. The early 20th century was a time of widespread racial segregation and limited opportunities for people of colour. Thorpe's participation in the Olympics was not just about personal glory; it was also about breaking barriers and challenging stereotypes.

The pentathlon, held over a single day, comprised five events: long jump, javelin throw, 200 metres, discus throw, and 1500 metres. Thorpe excelled from the start, demonstrating his all-around athletic ability. He won four of the five events, securing the gold medal and setting the stage for his performance in the decathlon. The decathlon, a two-day event, tested athletes in ten disciplines: 100 metres, long jump, shot put, high jump, 400 metres, 110 metres hurdles, discus throw, pole vault, javelin throw, and 1500 metres. Thorpe's performance in the decathlon was nothing short of extraordinary. He won four events outright and placed in the top four in all others, amassing a total of 8,412.95 points under the contemporary scoring system, a record that stood for decades.

Thorpe's dominance in both the pentathlon and decathlon was a testament to his incredible physical capabilities and his mental toughness. Competing against the best athletes in the world, he showcased a level of versatility and skill that was unprecedented. His ability to excel in such a diverse array of events highlighted not only his natural talent but also his rigorous training and determination.

The recognition of Thorpe's achievements at the 1912 Olympics was immediate and widespread. King Gustav V of Sweden, upon awarding Thorpe his medals, famously said, "You, sir, are the greatest athlete in the world." Thorpe's response, "Thanks, King," was characteristically modest, yet it underscored the significance of his accomplishment. Thorpe returned to the United States as a national hero, celebrated for his extraordinary feats.

However, Thorpe's triumph was soon overshadowed by controversy. In 1913, it was revealed that he had played semi-professional baseball before the Olympics, violating the strict amateurism rules of the time. Despite the fact that many athletes of the era engaged in similar activities without repercussion, Thorpe's medals were stripped, and his records were expunged from the official books. This decision was not only a personal blow to Thorpe but also a reflection of the racial and social prejudices that he faced throughout his life.

The aftermath of the medal controversy marked a difficult period for Thorpe. He continued to compete in various sports, including professional baseball and football, but the loss of his Olympic titles cast a long shadow over his career. Despite these challenges, Thorpe's resilience and determination never wavered. He became a symbol of perseverance and strength, continuing to inspire future generations of athletes.

Thorpe's legacy extended far beyond his athletic achievements. He became an advocate for Native American rights, using his platform to speak out against the injustices faced by his people. He also worked to promote sports among Native American youth, recognising the power of athletics to build confidence and break down barriers. Thorpe's contributions to society were multifaceted, encompassing not only his incredible sportsmanship but also his dedication to creating a more inclusive and equitable world.

The reinstatement of Thorpe's Olympic medals posthumously in 1983 was a long-overdue recognition of his contributions to sports and society. The decision acknowledged the unfairness of the original ruling and restored Thorpe's rightful place in Olympic history. This act of justice served as a reminder of the importance of challenging systemic discrimination and honouring those who have paved the way for future generations.

Thorpe's story is one of triumph over adversity, a narrative of an individual who rose above personal and societal challenges to achieve greatness. His performances at the 1912 Olympics remain a benchmark for athletic excellence, showcasing a level of versatility and skill that continues to inspire athletes around the world. Thorpe's legacy is a testament to the power of sport to transcend boundaries and bring people together, highlighting the enduring impact of his achievements.

The 1912 Olympics were a defining moment in Thorpe's life, but they were just one chapter in a remarkable story. His contributions to sports, society, and the fight for equality have left an indelible mark on history. Thorpe's journey from a small reservation in Oklahoma to the heights of Olympic glory is a powerful reminder of the potential within each individual to overcome obstacles and achieve greatness. His story continues to resonate, inspiring future generations to strive for excellence and justice in all aspects of life.

In reflecting on Thorpe's legacy, it is important to recognise the broader context of his achievements. His success came at a time when opportunities for people of colour were severely limited, and his accomplishments challenged the prevailing racial attitudes of the day. Thorpe's story is a testament to the resilience and determination required to overcome systemic barriers and achieve one's full potential. It is also a reminder of the ongoing struggle for equality and the importance of recognising and honouring the contributions of those who have fought for justice and inclusion.

Thorpe's impact on the world of sports is immeasurable. His performances set new standards for excellence and inspired countless athletes to push the boundaries of what is possible. His advocacy for Native American rights and his efforts to promote sports among indigenous youth have left a lasting legacy, highlighting the transformative power of athletics. Thorpe's story is a powerful reminder of the importance of perseverance, resilience, and the pursuit of justice, qualities that continue to inspire and guide us today.

As we celebrate Thorpe's achievements and reflect on his legacy, it is essential to honour his contributions and recognise the challenges he faced. His story is a testament to the power of the human spirit to overcome adversity and achieve greatness. Thorpe's legacy continues to inspire athletes, advocates, and individuals around the world, reminding us of the enduring impact of his remarkable journey.

Pele's World Cup Victories

Pelé's World Cup victories are an integral part of football history, defining an era of unparalleled excellence and establishing him as one of the greatest players the sport has ever seen. Born Edson Arantes do Nascimento in Três Corações, Brazil, in 1940, Pelé grew up in a modest household where his father, a former footballer, played a crucial role in nurturing his early passion for the game. By the age of 15, Pelé had joined Santos FC, where his prodigious talent quickly became evident, leading to his selection for the Brazilian national team at the remarkably young age of 16.

Pelé's first World Cup triumph came in 1958 in Sweden. The tournament was notable not only for Brazil's victory but also for Pelé's emergence on the world stage. Leading up to the World Cup, Pelé had already made headlines in Brazil with his remarkable performances for Santos. However, his inclusion in the national team was initially met with scepticism due to his youth. Nonetheless, the Brazilian squad, managed by Vicente Feola, was a formidable one, featuring stars like Didi, Garrincha, and Vavá. The team arrived in Sweden determined to shed their reputation for failing to win major international tournaments.

Pelé did not play in Brazil's first two matches due to a knee injury, but when he made his debut in the final group game against the Soviet Union, his impact was immediate. His presence boosted the team's morale and offensive capabilities. In the quarter-final against Wales, Pelé scored the only goal of the match, a brilliantly executed piece of skill that showcased his composure and precision. This goal made him the youngest scorer in World Cup history at 17 years and 239 days.

The semi-final against France saw Pelé truly announce himself to the world with a stunning hat-trick in Brazil's 5-2 victory. His goals demonstrated a combination of speed, skill, and clinical finishing that left the French defence bewildered. The final against the hosts, Sweden, was the ultimate stage for Pelé to showcase his talent. Brazil triumphed 5-2, with Pelé scoring twice. His first goal, an audacious flick over a defender followed by a volley, is still considered one of the greatest goals in World Cup history. Pelé's second goal was a perfectly timed header, capping off a remarkable tournament for the young forward. Brazil's victory in 1958 marked their first World Cup win and signified the arrival of a new footballing powerhouse.

The 1962 World Cup in Chile saw Pelé return with the Brazilian team, now considered favourites to retain their title. Managed by Aymoré Moreira, the squad was largely unchanged from 1958, boasting a blend of experience and youthful exuberance. Pelé started the tournament strongly, scoring a stunning solo goal against Mexico in Brazil's opening match. However, in the second match against Czechoslovakia, he suffered a severe injury that forced him to miss the rest of the tournament. Many thought Brazil's chances of retaining the title had diminished without their star player.

Despite Pelé's absence, Brazil's squad rose to the occasion. Garrincha, the mercurial winger, played a pivotal role, delivering several match-winning performances. In the quarter-finals against England, Garrincha scored twice in a 3-1 victory, while the semi-final against Chile saw him score another brace in a 4-2 win. Brazil faced Czechoslovakia in the final, and despite going a goal down early, they rallied to win 3-1, securing their second consecutive World Cup title. Pelé's injury had been a significant setback, but the team's depth and resilience ensured that they triumphed once again, further solidifying Brazil's status as a footballing juggernaut.

The 1966 World Cup in England was a challenging tournament for Pelé and Brazil. Expectations were high for the defending champions, but the team faced several obstacles. Pelé was targeted by rough tackles and aggressive defending, which took a toll on his performance and physical condition. In the opening match against Bulgaria, Pelé scored from a free-kick, becoming the first player to score in three different World Cups. However, he was injured during the game, forcing him to miss the next match against Hungary, which Brazil lost 3-1.

Pelé returned for the crucial group stage match against Portugal, but Brazil suffered another defeat, losing 3-1 and being eliminated from the tournament. The aggressive tactics employed by the opposition left Pelé battered and bruised, and he vowed never to play in another World Cup. Brazil's early exit was a major disappointment, but it also highlighted the need for better protection of skilful players like Pelé.

Pelé's decision to retire from World Cup football was short-lived, and he returned for the 1970 World Cup in Mexico, a tournament that would cement his legacy as the greatest player of all time. Managed by Mário Zagallo, Brazil's squad was arguably the most talented in history, featuring stars like Tostão, Jairzinho, Rivelino, and Carlos Alberto. The team played an attacking, free-flowing style of football that captivated fans around the world.

Pelé started the tournament with a goal in Brazil's 4-1 victory over Czechoslovakia, a powerful header that demonstrated his aerial prowess. In the match against England, Pelé's header was famously saved by Gordon Banks in what is often considered the greatest save in World Cup history. Despite being denied by Banks, Pelé's performances continued to dazzle. Against Romania, he scored twice in a 3-2 win, showcasing his skill and versatility.

Brazil's progression through the tournament was characterised by dominant performances and spectacular goals. In the quarter-finals against Peru, Brazil won 4-2, with Pelé providing crucial assists and demonstrating his vision and playmaking abilities. The semi-final against Uruguay saw Brazil recover from an early goal to win 3-1, with Pelé playing a key role in the team's attacking movements.

The final against Italy was the culmination of Pelé's World Cup journey. The match, played at the Estadio Azteca in Mexico City, was a showcase of Brazil's attacking brilliance. Pelé opened the scoring with a towering header, becoming the first player to score in four World Cups. His goal was the beginning of a masterclass in football from the Brazilian team. Brazil went on to win 4-1, with goals from Gerson, Jairzinho, and Carlos Alberto, whose thunderous strike capped off a sweeping team move orchestrated by Pelé. The victory secured Brazil's third World Cup title, and Pelé's contribution was instrumental.

Pelé's impact on the 1970 World Cup extended beyond his goals and assists. His leadership and experience were vital in guiding the team through the tournament. The 1970 World Cup is often regarded as the pinnacle of Pelé's career and a fitting conclusion to his World Cup journey. His performances were a testament to his extraordinary talent and his ability to shine on the biggest stage.

Pelé's World Cup victories had a profound impact on football and left an indelible mark on the sport's history. His success in 1958 as a teenager showcased his immense potential, while the triumph in 1962 demonstrated Brazil's depth and resilience. The challenges faced in 1966 highlighted the physical and tactical demands of the game, and the triumphant return in 1970 solidified Pelé's status as the greatest footballer of all time.

Beyond the trophies and accolades, Pelé's World Cup victories transcended the sport, inspiring millions around the world. His performances brought joy and pride to the people of Brazil, a country where football is deeply ingrained in the national identity. Pelé's ability to unite people through his talent and charisma made him a global icon, celebrated not only for his achievements on the pitch but also for his contributions to the sport and society.

Pelé's legacy is also defined by his sportsmanship and humility. Despite his immense success, he remained grounded and focused on using his platform to promote peace, education, and humanitarian causes. Pelé's influence extended beyond the football field, making him a beloved figure and an ambassador for the sport.

In reflecting on Pelé's World Cup victories, it is evident that his impact on football is immeasurable. His combination of skill, vision, and athleticism set new standards for excellence in the game. Pelé's ability to perform under pressure and deliver in crucial moments exemplified his greatness. His World Cup triumphs are a testament to his enduring legacy and the timeless appeal of his contributions to the sport.

As we celebrate Pelé's achievements, it is important to recognise the broader context of his career. His success came during a time of significant social and political change, and his influence extended beyond the boundaries of sport. Pelé's story is one of triumph over adversity, resilience, and the pursuit of greatness. His legacy continues to inspire future generations of footballers and fans, reminding us of the power of sport to bring people together and create lasting memories.

Pelé's World Cup victories are more than just milestones in a remarkable career; they are defining moments in the history of football. His performances on the world stage captured the imagination of millions and set a benchmark for excellence that continues to inspire. Pelé's legacy is a celebration of the beauty of the game and the enduring impact of a true footballing legend.

Secretariat's Triple Crown Win (1973)

Secretariat's Triple Crown win in 1973 remains one of the most iconic achievements in horse racing history, a story of remarkable athleticism, determination, and pure heart. Born on March 30, 1970, at Meadow Stable in Doswell, Virginia, Secretariat was sired by Bold Ruler and out of the mare Somethingroyal. From the beginning, Secretariat showed signs of exceptional talent, with his chestnut coat, powerful build, and commanding presence setting him apart.

Owned by Penny Chenery Tweedy, Secretariat's early training fell to Lucien Laurin, a seasoned horseman with a reputation for turning potential into performance. Ron Turcotte, a skilled jockey with a keen understanding of horses, became Secretariat's regular rider. Under Laurin and Turcotte's guidance, Secretariat began to develop into a formidable competitor. As a two-year-old, he quickly made a name for himself, winning races with a combination of speed, stamina, and an uncanny ability to accelerate when it mattered most.

By the end of 1972, Secretariat had become a household name in racing circles, securing the Eclipse Award for American Champion Two-Year-Old Male. The anticipation for his three-year-old season was immense. Secretariat's journey towards the Triple Crown began with high expectations, a blend of confidence and pressure that followed him into the 1973 racing season.

The first test came with the Kentucky Derby on May 5, 1973, at Churchill Downs. Known as "The Run for the Roses," the Derby is one of the most prestigious races, and winning it is a dream for any horse, trainer, or jockey. Secretariat entered the race as the favourite, his previous performances having earned him widespread acclaim. However, the field included other talented horses, particularly Sham, who was seen as a serious contender capable of challenging Secretariat's dominance.

Churchill Downs, with its grandstands packed and the atmosphere electric, provided the perfect stage. As the gates opened, Secretariat settled into the middle of the pack, a position that allowed him to conserve energy for his trademark late surge. Sham set a blistering pace early on, pushing the limits of endurance and speed. But as the race progressed, Secretariat began to show his true colours. Rounding the final turn, Secretariat unleashed an astonishing burst of speed, overtaking the leaders with ease. His powerful stride and unwavering determination saw him cross the finish line in a record time of 1:59 2/5, making him the first horse in history to complete the Derby in under two minutes. The victory was not just a win but a statement of his unmatched talent and potential.

Two weeks later, the journey continued with the Preakness Stakes at Pimlico Race Course in Baltimore, Maryland. The Preakness, shorter than the Derby, posed different challenges with its tighter turns and intense pace. Once again, Secretariat faced Sham and other strong competitors. The anticipation was palpable, with fans eager to see if Secretariat could take the next step towards the Triple Crown.

As the race began, Secretariat and Sham quickly positioned themselves at the front. What followed was one of the most memorable moments in racing history. Secretariat, in a display of sheer audacity and power, surged from last place to first on the backstretch, passing the entire field with what seemed like effortless ease. This extraordinary move left spectators and commentators in awe. Secretariat maintained his lead through the final turn and down the stretch, winning the Preakness by two and a half lengths. Although a timing error initially cast doubt on his record-breaking time, it was later confirmed that Secretariat had indeed set another record, further cementing his legendary status.

With victories in the Derby and Preakness, Secretariat stood on the brink of history. The final and most demanding challenge was the Belmont Stakes, held on June 9, 1973, at Belmont Park in Elmont, New York. The Belmont, at a mile and a half, is known as "The Test of the Champion" for its gruelling length that tests the stamina and endurance of even the greatest horses. Secretariat's preparation for the Belmont was meticulous, with Laurin ensuring that the colt was in peak condition.

Belmont Park was filled with an air of anticipation and excitement. Fans and experts alike gathered to witness what could be a historic moment. The question on everyone's mind was whether Secretariat could maintain his incredible form and complete the Triple Crown, a feat that had not been achieved in 25 years.

From the moment the gates opened, Secretariat took charge. Unlike in previous races, where he conserved energy early on, Secretariat set a blistering pace right from the start. His powerful strides quickly distanced him from the rest of the field. As the race progressed, the gap between Secretariat and the other horses widened to an almost unbelievable extent. By the time he reached the final turn, Secretariat was an astounding 31 lengths ahead. His jockey, Ron Turcotte, could barely believe the dominance he was experiencing. The crowd at Belmont Park erupted in cheers as Secretariat crossed the finish line in a record time of 2:24, smashing the previous record by an incredible margin. The victory was not just a win; it was a display of equine perfection, a performance that left an indelible mark on the sport.

Secretariat's Triple Crown win was the culmination of a journey filled with challenges and triumphs. Behind his success was a team of dedicated individuals who believed in his potential and worked tirelessly to bring out the best in him. Penny Chenery Tweedy's unwavering faith in Secretariat, Lucien Laurin's expert training, and Ron Turcotte's skilful riding were all crucial components of this remarkable achievement.

However, Secretariat's journey was not without adversity. Throughout his career, he faced intense scrutiny and pressure to perform at the highest level. The expectations placed on him were immense, and any misstep could have derailed his quest for greatness. Yet, Secretariat rose to the occasion time and again, displaying not just physical prowess but also a heart and spirit that resonated with fans around the world.

Secretariat's Triple Crown victory transcended the realm of horse racing, capturing the imagination of people from all walks of life. His performances were a testament to the beauty and power of the sport, showcasing the heights that can be achieved through talent, hard work, and determination. The legacy of Secretariat's Triple Crown win endures to this day, inspiring future generations of horses, trainers, jockeys, and racing enthusiasts.

In the years that followed, Secretariat continued to dominate the racing world, further solidifying his status as one of the greatest racehorses of all time. His impact on the sport extended beyond his racing career, influencing breeding practices and contributing to the development of future champions. Secretariat's legacy is a reminder of the extraordinary potential within every athlete, the importance of perseverance, and the magic that can occur when preparation meets opportunity.

Secretariat's Triple Crown win in 1973 remains a defining moment in the history of horse racing, a story of unmatched athleticism and heart.

From his early days at Meadow Stable to his record-breaking performances at Churchill Downs, Pimlico, and Belmont Park, Secretariat's journey is a testament to the enduring power of sport to inspire and uplift. His legacy continues to resonate, a beacon of excellence and a reminder of the greatness that can be achieved with dedication, passion, and a spirit that refuses to be broken.

The Immaculate Reception (1972)

The Immaculate Reception in 1972 is one of the most iconic moments in NFL history, a play that has transcended the sport to become a part of American cultural lore. The play occurred during the AFC Divisional Playoff game between the Pittsburgh Steelers and the Oakland Raiders on December 23, 1972, at Three Rivers Stadium in Pittsburgh. The Steelers, a team that had struggled for decades, were beginning to find their footing under head coach Chuck Noll, who had taken over the team in 1969. The Raiders, on the other hand, were a perennial powerhouse under the leadership of head coach John Madden.

The setting for this legendary play was the chilly confines of Three Rivers Stadium, a multipurpose venue that had become the home of the Steelers in 1970. The stadium was known for its harsh conditions, particularly in December, with cold winds sweeping through the stands. The atmosphere on that day was electric, as Pittsburgh fans, long-suffering and starved of success, packed the stadium in hopes of witnessing their team secure a rare playoff victory.

Leading up to the 1972 season, the Steelers were a team on the rise. After years of being the league's doormat, the franchise had begun to turn the corner under Noll's leadership. Key to this resurgence was the drafting of quarterback Terry Bradshaw in 1970, along with the acquisitions of future Hall of Famers like linebacker Jack Lambert and cornerback Mel Blount. The 1972 regular season had been a breakthrough for the Steelers, who finished with an 11-3 record and won the AFC Central Division title, earning a playoff berth for the first time since 1947.

The Raiders, meanwhile, were a seasoned and formidable team. Known for their physical and aggressive style of play, they had a reputation for toughness that was personified by players like linebacker Phil Villapiano and defensive tackle Otis Sistrunk. Under Madden's guidance, the Raiders had developed into one of the most consistent teams in the league, regularly contending for the championship.

As the game began, it was clear that it would be a hard-fought, defensive struggle. The Raiders struck first with a touchdown, and both defences dominated the early stages, with neither team able to establish a consistent offensive rhythm. The cold, wintry conditions made ball control difficult, and the game became a test of wills as much as skill. The Steelers' defence, anchored by the Steel Curtain front four, managed to keep the game within reach, limiting the Raiders' potent offense led by quarterback Ken Stabler.

Terry Bradshaw, the young and still somewhat erratic quarterback of the Steelers, faced immense pressure from the Raiders' relentless pass rush. His performance throughout the game was marked by moments of brilliance interspersed with near-disastrous mistakes. The Steelers' offense, however, managed to generate just enough momentum to stay in the contest, relying on the bruising running of Franco Harris and the reliable receiving of players like Frenchy Fuqua and Ron Shanklin.

As the fourth quarter wore on, the tension in the stadium became palpable. With time running out and the Raiders holding a 7-6 lead, it appeared that the Steelers' playoff hopes were slipping away. On their final possession, the Steelers found themselves facing a fourth-and-10 situation from their own 40-yard line. Bradshaw dropped back to pass, searching for an open receiver. Under heavy pressure, he launched a desperate throw downfield towards Fuqua. The pass seemed destined to fall incomplete or be intercepted, as Raiders safety Jack Tatum closed in on Fuqua.

What happened next would become the stuff of legend. As the ball reached Fuqua, he and Tatum collided violently, causing the ball to ricochet back through the air. In a split second that seemed to defy logic and the laws of physics, Franco Harris, the rookie running back who had been trailing the play, scooped the ball inches above the turf and sprinted towards the end zone. The stunned Raiders defenders, caught off guard by the unexpected turn of events, were unable to stop him. Harris crossed the goal line to give the Steelers an improbable 13-7 victory.

The aftermath of the play was chaotic and controversial. Initially, there was confusion about whether the touchdown would stand. According to NFL rules at the time, if an offensive player touched a forward pass and it then bounced to another offensive player without a defensive player touching it, the pass would be ruled incomplete. The officials huddled to discuss the play as the crowd waited in tense anticipation. After a lengthy deliberation, the referee signaled a touchdown, sending the stadium into a frenzy of jubilation.

Franco Harris, who had been drafted out of Penn State, had quickly become a fan favourite in Pittsburgh for his powerful running style and humble demeanor. His unlikely heroics in the Immaculate Reception cemented his place in Steelers lore and endeared him to the fans even further. The play itself was instantly dubbed the "Immaculate Reception," a term coined by a local fan and popularized by the media.

The Raiders, for their part, were left in disbelief. John Madden and his players vehemently argued that the ball had hit only Fuqua, making the reception illegal. Despite their protests, the play stood, and the Steelers advanced to the AFC Championship Game, where they ultimately fell to the Miami Dolphins.

The significance of the Immaculate Reception extended beyond the dramatic victory. For the Steelers, it marked the beginning of a dynasty that would dominate the NFL throughout the 1970s. The team went on to win four Super Bowl titles over the next decade, establishing themselves as one of the greatest franchises in sports history. The play symbolized the resilience and determination of the Steelers and their fans, embodying the blue-collar spirit of Pittsburgh.

The Immaculate Reception also highlighted the role of luck and serendipity in sports. The unlikely sequence of events that led to Harris's touchdown was a reminder that, no matter how meticulously a game is planned and executed, there is always an element of unpredictability. This aspect of the play has contributed to its enduring mystique and fascination.

For Franco Harris, the Immaculate Reception was a defining moment in a Hall of Fame career. He went on to become one of the most prolific running backs in NFL history, known for his durability, consistency, and ability to perform in clutch situations. Harris's calm and modest reaction to the play further endeared him to fans and teammates, who admired his humility and work ethic.

Terry Bradshaw's role in the Immaculate Reception was also pivotal. Despite the criticism he faced early in his career for his inconsistency, Bradshaw's leadership and arm strength were crucial to the Steelers' success. The pass he threw under immense pressure showcased his ability to make plays in critical moments, a trait that would become a hallmark of his career as he led the Steelers to four Super Bowl victories.

The Immaculate Reception has remained a subject of debate and discussion over the years. Various players, coaches, and analysts have offered differing interpretations of what exactly transpired in those fateful seconds. The play's legality, the officials' decision-making process, and the sheer improbability of the outcome have all been dissected and analyzed from multiple angles. This ongoing dialogue has only added to the legend of the Immaculate Reception, ensuring its place in the annals of NFL history.

In the broader context of sports, the Immaculate Reception is a testament to the power of unforgettable moments to shape the narrative of a team, a player, and even an entire city. The play encapsulates the drama, excitement, and emotional highs and lows that make sports a vital part of the human experience. For Steelers fans, it represents a turning point that transformed their team from perennial underachievers to champions, creating a legacy of excellence that continues to inspire new generations.

As the years have passed, the Immaculate Reception has been commemorated in various ways. Statues, plaques, and exhibits have been dedicated to the play and its key participants, ensuring that the memory of that December afternoon in 1972 remains vivid. The play is frequently featured in highlight reels, documentaries, and retrospectives, serving as a touchstone for discussions about the greatest moments in NFL history.

The enduring appeal of the Immaculate Reception lies in its combination of athletic brilliance, dramatic tension, and the element of the unexpected. It is a reminder that, in sports, anything can happen, and that the most memorable moments are often those that defy conventional expectations. Franco Harris's catch, born of quick reflexes and an instinctive understanding of the game, stands as a symbol of the extraordinary possibilities inherent in every play.

For the Oakland Raiders, the Immaculate Reception was a bitter pill to swallow. The team's disappointment and frustration were palpable, and the loss added fuel to the already intense rivalry between the Raiders and the Steelers. This rivalry, marked by hard-fought games and mutual respect, would become one of the defining features of the NFL in the 1970s, with both teams competing for supremacy in the AFC.

The legacy of the Immaculate Reception also reflects the broader cultural and social context of the early 1970s. The play occurred during a period of significant change and upheaval in American society, and the Steelers' rise to prominence mirrored the resilience and determination of a city undergoing its own transformation. Pittsburgh, once a hub of steel production, was facing economic challenges and an uncertain future. The success of the Steelers provided a source of pride and hope for the city's residents, reinforcing the idea that perseverance and hard work could overcome adversity.

The Immaculate Reception is more than just a football play; it is a defining moment in sports history that has left an indelible mark on the NFL and its fans. The combination of skill, luck, and drama that characterized Franco Harris's miraculous catch has ensured its place in the pantheon of great sports moments. As long as the game of football is played and celebrated, the memory of the Immaculate Reception will endure, inspiring fans and players alike with its timeless message of hope, resilience, and the magic of the unexpected.

Nadia Comaneci's Perfect 10 (1976 Olympics)

Nadia Comaneci's Perfect 10 at the 1976 Olympics stands as one of the most iconic moments in the history of gymnastics and the Olympic Games. Born on November 12, 1961, in Gheorgheni, Romania, Nadia Elena Comaneci showed exceptional talent in gymnastics from a very young age. Raised in the small town of Onești, she began training under the watchful eye of legendary coaches Béla and Márta Károlyi, who would later play pivotal roles in her journey to Olympic glory.

Comaneci's early years were marked by rigorous training and a fierce dedication to the sport. The Károlyis recognized her potential and developed a training regimen that focused on precision, discipline, and innovation. This intense preparation was set against the backdrop of Romania's state-sponsored sports system, which placed enormous pressure on athletes to succeed on the international stage. The country's communist regime saw sporting success as a means of demonstrating national superiority, and Comaneci's training was a testament to this philosophy.

In 1975, Comaneci made her mark on the international stage at the European Championships in Skien, Norway. She won four gold medals and one silver, demonstrating her exceptional skill and composure under pressure. These victories positioned her as a serious contender for the upcoming 1976 Summer Olympics in Montreal, Canada. As she prepared for the Olympics, Comaneci's routines were fine-tuned to perfection, with an emphasis on executing moves with flawless precision.

The setting for the 1976 Olympics was the Montreal Forum, a venue known for its capacity to host large-scale sporting events. The gymnastics competition attracted a global audience, eager to witness the performances of the world's best gymnasts. The atmosphere was charged with anticipation, as the spotlight turned to the young Romanian gymnast who had shown such promise in the lead-up to the Games.

Comaneci's journey to Olympic history began with the uneven bars, an event that would showcase her extraordinary talent. On July 18, 1976, she approached the apparatus with a calm demeanour that belied her age. Her routine was a complex series of moves performed with remarkable fluidity and grace. The audience watched in awe as Comaneci executed each element with flawless precision, culminating in a perfectly stuck dismount. When she finished, the silence turned to thunderous applause, as spectators sensed they had witnessed something special.

As the judges deliberated, the anticipation grew. When the score was finally displayed, it read 1.00. Confusion reigned briefly until it was clarified that the scoreboard, designed to show three digits, could not display a perfect 10.0. Nadia Comaneci had achieved the first perfect 10 in Olympic gymnastics history. The crowd erupted in applause and disbelief, while Comaneci remained composed, a testament to her discipline and focus.

This perfect 10 was not an isolated incident. Throughout the competition, Comaneci continued to demonstrate her mastery of the sport. On the balance beam, she performed with such poise and precision that she earned another perfect 10. Her routine included a series of acrobatic elements and graceful poses, all executed with flawless control. The beam, known for its difficulty and potential for error, seemed to present no challenge to Comaneci, who moved across it with the confidence of a seasoned champion.

In the floor exercise, Comaneci's routine combined elegance with athleticism. Her performance, set to the music of "Yes Sir, That's My Baby," showcased her artistic interpretation and technical prowess. Though she did not achieve a perfect 10 in this event, her score was still among the highest, contributing to her overall lead in the competition.

Comaneci's performance on the vault also earned her high marks. She executed her vaults with power and precision, landing each one with minimal deductions. Her ability to perform consistently across all apparatuses set her apart from her competitors and underscored her status as the leading gymnast of the Games.

The all-around competition, which tests a gymnast's skill across all four apparatuses, was the ultimate measure of Comaneci's dominance. Her combined scores from the uneven bars, balance beam, floor exercise, and vault placed her firmly at the top of the leaderboard. By the end of the competition, Comaneci had secured three gold medals (all-around, uneven bars, and balance beam), one silver (team competition), and one bronze (floor exercise), solidifying her place in Olympic history.

Nadia Comaneci's achievements at the 1976 Olympics were not just a triumph of athletic ability, but also a demonstration of extraordinary mental strength. The pressure to perform at such a high level, under the watchful eyes of the world, was immense. Comaneci's ability to maintain her composure and deliver flawless routines time and again was a testament to her discipline and mental fortitude.

The impact of Comaneci's perfect 10 extended beyond the realm of gymnastics. Her performances captivated audiences worldwide and brought unprecedented attention to the sport. She became an international sensation, with her image gracing magazine covers and her story inspiring countless young gymnasts. The perfection she achieved in Montreal set a new standard for the sport, influencing the training and aspirations of future generations of gymnasts.

In the years following her Olympic triumph, Comaneci continued to compete at the highest level, winning numerous national and international titles. However, her relationship with her coaches, particularly Béla Károlyi, became strained. The intense training and pressure to succeed took a toll on her physically and emotionally. Despite these challenges, Comaneci's legacy as a pioneer in gymnastics remained intact.

Nadia Comaneci's journey was not without its adversities. Growing up in a country with a strict and demanding sports system, she faced immense pressure to perform and succeed. The rigorous training and the high expectations placed upon her required not only physical endurance but also mental resilience. Her ability to navigate these challenges and emerge as a champion is a testament to her strength of character.

Comaneci's impact on gymnastics can still be felt today. Her perfect 10s set a benchmark that gymnasts strive to reach, and her style and technique have influenced the evolution of the sport. The scoring system in gymnastics has since been revised, partly in response to the perfection she demonstrated, to accommodate the increasing difficulty and complexity of modern routines.

The legacy of Nadia Comaneci's perfect 10 at the 1976 Olympics is one of inspiration and excellence. Her performances in Montreal remain a gold standard in gymnastics, a reminder of what can be achieved through dedication, hard work, and a relentless pursuit of perfection. Comaneci's achievements continue to inspire athletes around the world, reminding them that the pursuit of excellence is a journey that transcends the boundaries of sport. Her story is a celebration of the human spirit and its capacity to reach new heights in the face of adversity.

The Battle of the Sexes (1973)

The Battle of the Sexes in 1973 was more than just a tennis match; it was a cultural spectacle that encapsulated the social dynamics and gender politics of the era. The protagonists of this historic event were Billie Jean King, a leading figure in women's tennis, and Bobby Riggs, a former Wimbledon champion and self-proclaimed male chauvinist. The match took place on September 20, 1973, at the Houston Astrodome in Texas, and it symbolised the ongoing struggle for gender equality in sports and society at large.

Billie Jean King, born on November 22, 1943, in Long Beach, California, was a trailblazer in women's tennis. From an early age, King displayed exceptional talent and a fierce determination to excel. She turned professional in the early 1960s and quickly rose to prominence, winning numerous Grand Slam titles. King was not just a champion on the court; she was also a vocal advocate for women's rights and gender equality. Her efforts extended beyond tennis, as she fought for equal prize money, better playing conditions, and greater respect for female athletes.

Bobby Riggs, on the other hand, was born on February 25, 1918, in Los Angeles, California. Riggs had a distinguished career in the 1940s, winning Wimbledon and several other major titles. By the 1970s, Riggs was retired from professional tennis but remained a prominent figure in the sport. Known for his gambling and flamboyant personality, Riggs saw an opportunity to capitalise on the growing women's liberation movement by challenging top female players to matches. He believed that women could never compete with men on an equal footing and sought to prove his point through a series of high-profile challenges.

The backdrop to the Battle of the Sexes was the broader women's rights movement of the 1960s and 1970s. This period saw significant strides towards gender equality, with women advocating for equal opportunities, fair pay, and the end of discriminatory practices. Title IX, passed in 1972, was a landmark piece of legislation that prohibited gender discrimination in federally funded educational programs and activities, including sports. The legislation was a significant victory for women's athletics, leading to increased funding and opportunities for female athletes at the collegiate level.

In this context, Bobby Riggs initially challenged Margaret Court, the world's number one women's player at the time. The match, dubbed the "Mother's Day Massacre," took place on May 13, 1973. Riggs, at 55 years old, used his experience and cunning to defeat Court in straight sets, 6-2, 6-1. This victory bolstered Riggs' claims of male superiority in tennis and set the stage for an even bigger challenge: a match against Billie Jean King.

King initially resisted Riggs' provocations, recognising that such a match could either bolster or undermine the women's movement depending on the outcome. However, after Riggs' victory over Court and his continued taunting, King decided to accept the challenge. She saw it as an opportunity to strike a blow for women's equality and to demonstrate that women could compete at the highest levels against men.

The Houston Astrodome, an indoor stadium known for hosting a variety of major sporting events, was chosen as the venue for the match. The event was promoted heavily, drawing immense media attention and anticipation. The atmosphere on the day of the match was electric, with over 30,000 spectators in attendance and millions more watching on television around the world. The stage was set for a historic showdown, one that transcended the sport of tennis.

King approached the match with a strategic mindset, understanding that Riggs' style of play relied heavily on psychological tactics and a steady, consistent game. Riggs, confident in his ability to outsmart and outplay King, entered the match with his characteristic bravado, wearing a "Sugar Daddy" jacket and arriving in a rickshaw pulled by young women. King, however, was focused and determined. She trained rigorously in the weeks leading up to the match, honing her skills and preparing both physically and mentally for the challenge.

As the match began, it quickly became apparent that King was not intimidated by Riggs' antics. She played aggressively from the start, using her powerful serve and precise groundstrokes to dominate the exchanges. Riggs, unable to cope with King's pace and intensity, struggled to find his rhythm. King took the first set 6-4, setting the tone for the rest of the match. Riggs tried to adjust his strategy, but King continued to press her advantage, showcasing her superior fitness and tactical acumen. She won the second set 6-3, moving closer to a historic victory.

The third set saw King maintain her momentum, exploiting Riggs' weaknesses and forcing him into errors. Riggs, visibly frustrated and fatigued, could not mount a comeback. King closed out the match with a 6-3 victory in the final set, securing a straight-sets win. The crowd erupted in applause, and King was carried off the court in celebration. Her triumph was not just a personal victory; it was a significant moment for the women's rights movement, challenging outdated notions of gender superiority in sports.

The aftermath of the Battle of the Sexes had a profound impact on both tennis and society. King's victory was celebrated as a landmark achievement for gender equality, inspiring women across the globe to pursue their dreams and assert their rights. The match helped to elevate the status of women's tennis, leading to increased sponsorship, media coverage, and prize money. King continued her advocacy for gender equality, founding the Women's Tennis Association (WTA) and working tirelessly to ensure equal opportunities for female athletes.

For Bobby Riggs, the defeat was a humbling experience. While he continued to promote himself and engage in various publicity stunts, his claims of male superiority were significantly undermined by the loss. Riggs maintained a sense of humour about the match, acknowledging King's superior performance and the broader significance of the event.

The Battle of the Sexes remains a defining moment in sports history, illustrating the power of competition to challenge societal norms and promote equality. King's victory was a testament to her skill, determination, and courage, as well as a significant step forward in the ongoing struggle for gender equality. The match demonstrated that women could compete on equal terms with men, both on and off the court, and it continues to inspire new generations of athletes and advocates.

Simone Biles' Dominance in Gymnastics

Simone Biles' dominance in gymnastics is a story of extraordinary talent, unparalleled dedication, and remarkable resilience. Born on March 14, 1997, in Columbus, Ohio, Biles faced significant challenges early in life. Her biological mother struggled with substance abuse, leading to Simone and her siblings being placed in foster care. At the age of six, she and her younger sister were adopted by their maternal grandfather, Ron Biles, and his wife, Nellie. This new environment provided the stability and support that would be crucial for Simone's future success.

Simone's journey in gymnastics began when she was six years old. During a daycare field trip to Bannon's Gymnastix, she imitated the gymnasts she watched and was soon encouraged to pursue the sport. Her natural aptitude was evident from the start. The coaches quickly recognised her potential, and she began training under Aimee Boorman, who would become a key figure in her career. Boorman's guidance helped Simone develop her skills and fostered a supportive and positive atmosphere, crucial for a young athlete with such immense talent.

As Simone progressed through the levels of gymnastics, her performances became increasingly impressive. By the age of 14, she had made her mark on the national stage, earning a place on the Junior National Team. Her unique combination of power, agility, and precision set her apart from her peers. Simone's routines were marked by a high degree of difficulty, executed with remarkable consistency. This early promise foreshadowed her dominance in the sport.

Simone's breakthrough came in 2013 when she competed in the Senior National Championships. At just 16, she won the all-around title, showcasing her extraordinary skills on all apparatuses. This victory earned her a spot on the U.S. team for the World Championships in Antwerp, Belgium. The competition was a turning point. Simone won gold in the all-around, floor exercise, and silver on vault, firmly establishing herself as the world's leading gymnast. Her performances were characterised by difficult elements executed with flawless technique, a hallmark of her style.

The 2014 and 2015 World Championships solidified Simone's status as the dominant force in gymnastics. In 2014, she defended her all-around title and added gold medals on the balance beam and floor exercise, as well as a silver on vault and a bronze on uneven bars. The following year, she again won the all-around, balance beam, and floor exercise titles, further extending her legacy. Simone's ability to maintain such a high level of performance across multiple disciplines was unprecedented. Her routines included innovative elements that pushed the boundaries of the sport, earning her admiration and respect from the gymnastics community.

In the lead-up to the 2016 Rio Olympics, expectations for Simone were sky-high. She had dominated every competition she entered and was widely regarded as the favourite for multiple gold medals. The Olympic Games provided a global stage for Simone to showcase her extraordinary talent. Her performances in Rio did not disappoint. She won gold medals in the all-around, team competition, vault, and floor exercise, as well as a bronze on the balance beam. Simone's execution was nearly flawless, with her routines featuring a combination of power, grace, and precision that left audiences in awe.

Simone's success in Rio catapulted her to international stardom. She became a role model for aspiring gymnasts and an inspiration to many. Her achievements highlighted the importance of dedication, hard work, and resilience. Despite the pressures of fame and high expectations, Simone remained focused on her goals and continued to push the limits of what was possible in gymnastics.

Following the 2016 Olympics, Simone took a brief hiatus from competition to focus on her personal life and explore other opportunities. She participated in the television show "Dancing with the Stars," where her competitive spirit and athletic prowess were once again on display. During this time, she also reflected on her career and the challenges she had faced. Simone's journey was not without adversity. She had to navigate the pressures of elite competition, public scrutiny, and personal struggles, including her experience with the USA Gymnastics abuse scandal.

In 2018, Simone made a triumphant return to competition. At the U.S. National Championships, she won her fifth all-around title, a record in the modern era. Her performances were characterised by even greater difficulty and execution, showcasing her continued evolution as a gymnast. Later that year, at the World Championships in Doha, Qatar, she further cemented her legacy by winning four gold medals and a bronze, despite competing with a kidney stone. Simone's resilience and determination were on full display, as she overcame physical and mental challenges to achieve success.

The following year, at the 2019 World Championships in Stuttgart, Germany, Simone continued to dominate. She won five gold medals, bringing her total World Championship medal count to 25, the most of any gymnast in history. Her routines included several new elements, some of which were named after her, such as the "Biles" on floor exercise and the "Biles II" on vault. These innovative skills demonstrated Simone's commitment to pushing the boundaries of the sport and her desire to continually improve.

As the Tokyo 2020 Olympics approached, Simone was once again the favourite to win multiple gold medals. However, the COVID-19 pandemic forced the postponement of the Games, adding an additional year of preparation and uncertainty. Despite these challenges, Simone remained focused on her training and continued to perform at an exceptionally high level.

In Tokyo, Simone faced an unexpected challenge when she withdrew from several events due to mental health concerns. Her decision to prioritise her well-being over competition was widely praised and sparked important conversations about mental health in sports. Simone's courage in addressing her struggles publicly demonstrated her leadership and commitment to advocating for athlete well-being.

Despite these challenges, Simone competed in the balance beam final, where she won a bronze medal. Her performance was a testament to her resilience and determination, showcasing her ability to overcome adversity and continue to excel at the highest level. Simone's experiences in Tokyo highlighted the importance of mental health and self-care, further solidifying her status as a role model and advocate for athletes.

Simone Biles' dominance in gymnastics is not just about her incredible achievements and record-breaking performances. It is also about her journey, the challenges she has faced, and the impact she has had on the sport and society. Her story is one of extraordinary talent, relentless dedication, and remarkable resilience. Simone's ability to continually push the limits of what is possible in gymnastics has inspired countless athletes and fans around the world. Her legacy will be remembered not only for her medals and titles but also for her courage, advocacy, and the positive change she has brought to the sport.

Simone's influence extends beyond the gym. She has used her platform to speak out on important issues, including racial equality, gender equality, and mental health. Her advocacy has helped to raise awareness and drive positive change, making her a powerful voice for social justice. Simone's impact on the sport of gymnastics and society as a whole is profound, and her legacy will continue to inspire future generations.

Simone Biles' dominance in gymnastics is a story of unparalleled talent, dedication, and resilience. Her achievements have set new standards for the sport, and her journey has inspired countless individuals around the world. Simone's legacy is a testament to the power of hard work, determination, and the courage to overcome adversity. As she continues to push the boundaries of what is possible in gymnastics, Simone Biles will be remembered as one of the greatest athletes of all time.

Wilt Chamberlain's 100-Point Game (1962)

Wilt Chamberlain's 100-point game on March 2, 1962, remains one of the most extraordinary achievements in the history of professional basketball. Born on August 21, 1936, in Philadelphia, Pennsylvania, Chamberlain grew up in a time when basketball was still evolving as a sport. His physical stature, standing at 7 feet 1 inch, and his extraordinary athletic ability set him apart from his peers at an early age. Chamberlain's basketball journey began at Overbrook High School in Philadelphia, where he quickly became a local legend, dominating games and breaking records with ease.

After high school, Chamberlain attended the University of Kansas, where he continued to excel, leading the Jayhawks to the NCAA championship game in 1957. His collegiate career was marked by remarkable performances and a constant battle against double and triple teams, as opponents desperately tried to contain his dominance. Following his college career, Chamberlain joined the Harlem Globetrotters for a year before entering the NBA.

Chamberlain's professional career began with the Philadelphia Warriors in 1959, and he made an immediate impact, winning the Rookie of the Year and the MVP award in his first season. His scoring ability, combined with his rebounding and defensive prowess, made him one of the most formidable players in the league. By the time the 1961-62 season arrived, Chamberlain had already established himself as a force of nature, capable of putting up astronomical numbers on any given night.

The setting for Chamberlain's historic 100-point game was Hershey Sports Arena in Hershey, Pennsylvania, a modest venue compared to the larger arenas of the NBA. The Philadelphia Warriors were hosting the New York Knicks in a relatively low-profile game, not even broadcast on television. The arena, primarily used for ice hockey, had a seating capacity of about 8,000, though only a fraction of that number was in attendance. The game was a part of the Warriors' efforts to expand their fan base by playing in various locations around Pennsylvania.

Leading up to the game, Chamberlain had been on an incredible scoring streak, routinely putting up 50-point games and breaking records with regularity. His endurance and stamina were legendary; he often played the entire game without rest. Chamberlain's extraordinary physical condition allowed him to maintain a high level of performance throughout the grueling NBA schedule. His scoring feats were complemented by his ability to dominate the boards, often grabbing 20 to 30 rebounds a game.

The game against the Knicks began like many others, with Chamberlain asserting his dominance early. From the opening tip, it was clear that the Knicks had no answer for his combination of size, strength, and skill. Chamberlain scored effortlessly, utilizing a variety of moves in the post, powerful dunks, and surprisingly accurate mid-range shots. His teammates, recognising the potential for something special, began feeding him the ball at every opportunity.

By halftime, Chamberlain had already scored 41 points, a remarkable total for most players but not unprecedented for him. The second half saw Chamberlain intensify his efforts. The Warriors, sensing history in the making, continued to run their offense through him. The Knicks, despite their best efforts, could do little to stop him. They tried double-teaming and even triple-teaming him, but Chamberlain's sheer physicality and skill allowed him to score over and around them with ease.

As Chamberlain's point total climbed, the crowd and his teammates became increasingly aware that something extraordinary was happening. The atmosphere in the arena grew electric, with each basket met by louder and louder cheers. By the end of the third quarter, Chamberlain had scored 69 points, already surpassing his previous career high. The focus of the game shifted entirely to Chamberlain's pursuit of 100 points.

The fourth quarter was a frenetic display of offensive basketball, with the Warriors doing everything in their power to get Chamberlain the ball. The Knicks, realising the historic nature of the moment, tried desperately to prevent him from reaching the milestone. They fouled other Warriors players intentionally, hoping to slow down the game and deny Chamberlain scoring opportunities. However, the strategy only served to further fuel the Warriors' determination.

Chamberlain continued to score, often in spectacular fashion. His teammates, including Guy Rodgers and Al Attles, worked tirelessly to get him the ball in scoring positions. Chamberlain's endurance was on full display as he powered through fatigue, determined to reach the century mark. With less than a minute remaining, Chamberlain scored his 98th point, and the anticipation in the arena reached a fever pitch.

Then, with just 46 seconds left on the clock, Chamberlain took a pass from Joe Ruklick and laid the ball in to reach 100 points. The arena erupted in celebration, and the game was momentarily stopped as fans and teammates rushed the court to congratulate him. Chamberlain's achievement was unprecedented and remains unmatched in the annals of professional basketball. The final score of the game was 169-147 in favour of the Warriors, but the result was secondary to the historic accomplishment of their star player.

Chamberlain's 100-point game was more than just a display of individual brilliance; it was a testament to his resilience and competitive spirit. Despite facing constant physical and mental challenges throughout his career, Chamberlain consistently pushed the boundaries of what was possible in the sport. His performance in Hershey was the culmination of years of hard work, dedication, and an unrelenting desire to be the best.

The aftermath of Chamberlain's historic game saw widespread recognition and admiration for his achievement. Newspapers across the country highlighted his 100-point game, and it quickly became a defining moment in NBA history. Chamberlain's performance helped to elevate the profile of the league, attracting new fans and increasing interest in professional basketball.

Chamberlain's dominance continued throughout his career, as he went on to break numerous records and win multiple MVP awards. His rivalry with Bill Russell of the Boston Celtics became one of the most storied matchups in sports history, pitting Chamberlain's scoring and rebounding prowess against Russell's defensive brilliance and team success. Despite often being overshadowed by the Celtics' dynasty, Chamberlain's individual achievements remained unparalleled.

Off the court, Chamberlain was known for his charismatic personality and varied interests. He pursued a range of activities, including acting, writing, and even professional volleyball. His multifaceted life and towering presence made him a larger-than-life figure in American sports and popular culture.

Chamberlain's legacy is not defined solely by his 100-point game, but by his overall impact on the sport of basketball. His influence can be seen in the way the game is played today, with an emphasis on athleticism, versatility, and scoring ability. Chamberlain's records, many of which still stand, serve as benchmarks for greatness in the NBA.

The story of Wilt Chamberlain's 100-point game is a testament to the heights that can be reached through talent, determination, and an unyielding competitive spirit. It remains one of the most celebrated achievements in sports history, a milestone that continues to inspire and captivate fans and athletes alike. Chamberlain's performance on that fateful night in Hershey is a reminder of the extraordinary potential of human athleticism and the enduring power of sports to create moments of lasting significance.

Eric Liddell's 1924 Olympic Gold

Eric Liddell's victory at the 1924 Paris Olympics is a tale of unwavering faith, exceptional athleticism, and the triumph of the human spirit. Born on January 16, 1902, in Tientsin (now Tianjin), China, Liddell was the son of Scottish missionaries. His upbringing was marked by a deep commitment to Christianity and a strong sense of discipline, qualities that would profoundly influence his life and career. At the age of six, Liddell was sent to Eltham College, a boarding school in London, where he began to display his remarkable talent for sports. By the time he moved to Edinburgh University, his prowess in rugby and athletics was well established.

Liddell's athletic journey gained momentum at Edinburgh University, where he studied Pure Science. His performance in the 100 yards and 220 yards sprints earned him widespread recognition. Known for his distinctive running style, characterised by a high head tilt and flailing arms, Liddell's speed and determination set him apart from his contemporaries. His reputation grew rapidly, and by the early 1920s, he was considered one of Britain's top sprinters. His deep religious convictions were integral to his identity, and he became renowned not just for his athletic ability, but also for his unwavering commitment to his faith.

The 1924 Paris Olympics were eagerly anticipated, with athletes from around the world gathering to compete on the grandest stage. The British team was strong, featuring Liddell and Harold Abrahams, another prominent sprinter. Liddell's main event was the 100 metres, but controversy arose when he discovered that the heats were scheduled for a Sunday. Liddell, a devout Christian, refused to compete on the Sabbath, adhering to his belief that Sunday should be a day of rest and worship. This decision shocked many, as the 100 metres was his best event and he was a favourite to win gold.

Despite the immense pressure from the British Olympic Committee and the public, Liddell stood firm in his convictions. His decision was widely debated, with some questioning his commitment to his country and his team. However, Liddell's resolve was unshaken, and he chose to compete in the 400 metres instead, an event for which he was not a favourite. The 400 metres required different training and strategy, but Liddell's athletic versatility and determination propelled him forward.

The setting for the 1924 Olympics was the Stade Olympique Yves-du-Manoir in Colombes, a suburb of Paris. The stadium, newly built for the Games, could hold up to 45,000 spectators and was a symbol of modernity and sporting excellence. The atmosphere was electric, with athletes and spectators from around the world coming together to witness the pinnacle of sporting achievement. The pressure was immense, particularly for Liddell, who was stepping into an unfamiliar event under the weight of immense expectations.

Leading up to the 400 metres race, Liddell's training was intense. His coach, Tom McKerchar, devised a regimen to build his endurance and speed for the longer distance. Despite the challenges, Liddell approached the race with characteristic humility and faith. On the day of the race, July 11, 1924, the tension was palpable. Liddell faced a formidable field of competitors, including the American favourites Horatio Fitch and J. Douglas MacLachlan, both renowned for their prowess in the 400 metres.

As the race began, Liddell surged forward with his trademark style, defying conventional sprinting techniques. His head was tilted back, and his arms flailed, but his speed and power were undeniable. He took an early lead, maintaining a blistering pace. The crowd watched in awe as Liddell's determination drove him forward. Despite the longer distance, he maintained his lead, and as he approached the final stretch, it became clear that he was on the verge of a historic victory.

Liddell crossed the finish line in 47.6 seconds, breaking the existing Olympic record. His performance was not just a testament to his physical prowess, but also to his faith and determination. The victory was a moment of immense triumph, celebrated by spectators and athletes alike. Liddell's gold medal in the 400 metres was a defining moment of the 1924 Olympics, symbolising the power of conviction and the spirit of the Games.

After his victory, Liddell continued to compete in the 200 metres, where he won a bronze medal, further solidifying his status as one of Britain's greatest athletes. His achievements in Paris were widely celebrated, and he returned to Britain as a national hero. Despite the accolades and fame, Liddell remained humble and committed to his faith. He saw his athletic success as a platform to share his beliefs and inspire others.

Following the Olympics, Liddell's life took a different direction. He graduated from Edinburgh University and chose to follow in his parents' footsteps, becoming a missionary in China. His commitment to his faith led him to a life of service, teaching and preaching in rural communities. Despite the challenges and dangers of missionary work, Liddell remained dedicated to his mission, providing education and spiritual guidance to those in need.

Liddell's time in China was marked by both triumph and adversity. He married Florence Mackenzie, a fellow missionary, and they had three daughters. However, the political situation in China was becoming increasingly unstable, with the Japanese invasion during World War II bringing significant hardship. Liddell continued his work, even as the dangers grew. His faith and commitment to helping others remained unwavering.

In 1943, Liddell was interned in a Japanese civilian internment camp in Weihsien, China. Despite the harsh conditions, Liddell continued to teach and support his fellow internees, becoming a source of inspiration and hope. His health deteriorated under the brutal conditions, and in February 1945, he died of a brain tumour, just months before the end of the war. His death was a profound loss, but his legacy of faith, humility, and athletic excellence endured.

Liddell's story is a testament to the power of conviction and the human spirit. His achievements on the track were remarkable, but it was his character and faith that truly set him apart. His decision to forgo the 100 metres at the 1924 Olympics, despite the immense pressure, was a defining moment that showcased his unwavering principles. His subsequent victory in the 400 metres was a triumph of both athletic ability and personal integrity.

The legacy of Eric Liddell continues to inspire athletes and individuals around the world. His life story was famously depicted in the 1981 film "Chariots of Fire," which brought his remarkable achievements and character to a new generation. The film's portrayal of Liddell's journey captured the essence of his spirit and the profound impact of his faith and determination.

Liddell's impact extends beyond his athletic achievements. His commitment to serving others and his dedication to his faith left a lasting legacy in the communities he touched. His story is a reminder of the power of principles and the importance of staying true to one's beliefs, even in the face of immense pressure and adversity.

Eric Liddell's 1924 gold medal victory stands as a symbol of the triumph of the human spirit. His journey from the mission fields of China to the Olympic podium in Paris is a testament to the enduring power of faith, determination, and humility. Liddell's legacy continues to inspire, reminding us that true greatness is not just measured by medals and records, but by the character and principles that guide us.

Michael Jordan's Flu Game (1997 NBA Finals)

Michael Jordan's Flu Game during the 1997 NBA Finals is one of the most legendary performances in basketball history. The story of this game is a testament to Jordan's extraordinary talent, unparalleled determination, and relentless competitive spirit. Born on February 17, 1963, in Brooklyn, New York, Jordan grew up in Wilmington, North Carolina, where he developed his love for basketball. His journey to the NBA was marked by hard work, perseverance, and an unyielding drive to be the best. By the time the 1997 Finals rolled around, Jordan had already established himself as the greatest player of his generation, if not of all time.

The Chicago Bulls, led by Jordan, were in the midst of their second three-peat, having won the championship in 1991, 1992, and 1993, and again in 1996. The 1996-97 season saw the Bulls finishing with a league-best 69-13 record, showcasing their dominance. The Utah Jazz, led by Karl Malone and John Stockton, were the Bulls' formidable opponents in the Finals. The Jazz had also enjoyed a stellar season, finishing with a 64-18 record and securing the Western Conference title.

As the Finals began, the stage was set for a thrilling showdown between two of the league's best teams. The Bulls took an early lead by winning Game 1, but the Jazz responded by taking Game 2. The series shifted to Utah, where the Jazz won Game 3, putting the Bulls in a precarious position. Game 4 saw Jordan and the Bulls bounce back, tying the series at 2-2. With the series now effectively a best-of-three, Game 5 in Utah became a pivotal contest.

The night before Game 5, Jordan's condition took a dramatic turn for the worse. He was struck by severe flu-like symptoms, later speculated to be food poisoning. Despite receiving medical attention throughout the night, his condition did not improve. Jordan was extremely weak and dehydrated, with team doctors advising him against playing. However, Jordan's competitive nature would not allow him to sit out such a crucial game. His will to win and his commitment to his team compelled him to take the court.

The Delta Center in Salt Lake City was filled to capacity with 19,911 fervent Jazz fans, hoping to see their team take control of the series. The atmosphere was electric, with the crowd's energy reflecting the high stakes of the game. The challenge for Jordan was immense, facing not only the physical demands of the game but also the hostile environment of the Delta Center.

As the game began, it was evident that Jordan was not his usual self. He moved slowly and appeared visibly fatigued. The Jazz capitalised on this, jumping out to an early lead. The Bulls struggled to find their rhythm, and it looked like the Jazz might run away with the game. However, as the first quarter progressed, Jordan began to find his footing. Despite the obvious physical discomfort, he started to make key plays, scoring points and setting up his teammates.

Throughout the game, Jordan's condition visibly deteriorated, but his performance did not. He summoned reserves of strength and willpower that defied his physical state. His teammates, recognising the gravity of the situation, rallied around him. Scottie Pippen, Jordan's right-hand man, played a crucial role, providing support both on the court and emotionally. The Bulls' bench also stepped up, understanding the need to relieve some of the pressure from Jordan.

The second quarter saw Jordan scoring with a mix of jump shots, layups, and free throws. He continued to push through his illness, demonstrating incredible stamina and mental toughness. The Jazz, led by Malone and Stockton, maintained their aggressive play, but the Bulls matched their intensity. By halftime, the game was tightly contested, with the Bulls trailing by a narrow margin.

The third quarter was a testament to Jordan's indomitable spirit. He carried the Bulls on his back, scoring 17 points in the period. His performance was a combination of skill, tenacity, and sheer willpower. Each basket he made seemed to deflate the Jazz and energise his teammates. Despite being visibly exhausted, Jordan refused to relent, pushing himself to the limits of his endurance.

In the fourth quarter, the game remained close, with both teams trading leads. The physical toll on Jordan was apparent, yet he continued to play with remarkable intensity. Every time the Jazz threatened to pull away, Jordan responded with crucial baskets or defensive plays. His leadership on the court was undeniable, inspiring his teammates to elevate their game.

With the game tied in the final minutes, Jordan delivered one of the most iconic sequences of his career. He made a critical three-pointer to give the Bulls a lead. This shot, made with just under a minute remaining, showcased his ability to perform under immense pressure. The Jazz tried to respond, but the Bulls' defence held firm. Jordan's crucial free throws in the dying seconds sealed the victory for the Bulls, who won 90-88.

Jordan finished the game with 38 points, 7 rebounds, 5 assists, 3 steals, and 1 block. His performance, under the circumstances, was nothing short of miraculous. As the final buzzer sounded, Jordan collapsed into Pippen's arms, exhausted but triumphant. The image of Pippen helping the physically drained Jordan off the court became one of the defining moments of the 1997 Finals.

The significance of the Flu Game extended beyond the box score. It epitomised the essence of Michael Jordan's career – his relentless drive, his refusal to accept defeat, and his ability to elevate his performance in the most challenging circumstances. Jordan's heroics in Game 5 were a testament to his extraordinary competitive spirit and his status as one of the greatest athletes of all time.

The Bulls went on to win Game 6 in Chicago, clinching their fifth NBA championship. Jordan was named Finals MVP, a recognition of his outstanding performances throughout the series, particularly in the Flu Game. His ability to overcome such adversity and deliver one of the greatest performances in NBA history further cemented his legacy.

The Flu Game is often cited as a prime example of Jordan's legendary status and his unparalleled will to win. It has become a part of basketball folklore, a story that encapsulates the greatness of Michael Jordan. The narrative of Jordan battling illness and leading his team to victory resonates with fans and athletes alike, symbolising the determination and resilience that define true champions.

Jordan's career was filled with countless memorable moments and achievements, but the Flu Game holds a special place in the hearts of basketball fans. It is a reminder of his remarkable physical and mental attributes, his leadership, and his unwavering commitment to excellence. The legacy of the Flu Game continues to inspire and captivate, serving as a testament to the greatness of Michael Jordan and the enduring allure of sport.

The New Zealand All Blacks Haka

The New Zealand All Blacks' Haka is one of the most iconic and recognisable traditions in the world of sports. This traditional Māori war dance is performed by the national rugby team of New Zealand before every match, serving as a powerful display of unity, strength, and cultural pride. The origins of the Haka trace back to the indigenous Māori people of New Zealand, where it was used to intimidate opponents and demonstrate the strength and cohesion of a tribe. The All Blacks' adoption of the Haka has transformed it into a symbol of national identity and an integral part of their pre-match ritual.

The Māori culture, deeply rooted in the history of New Zealand, is rich with traditions, stories, and customs that have been passed down through generations. The Haka, in particular, is a vital part of this heritage. Traditionally, the Haka was performed by warriors before a battle to intimidate the enemy and to summon the strength and unity of the tribe. It is characterised by vigorous movements, rhythmic chanting, and fierce facial expressions, creating an awe-inspiring spectacle. The words and movements of the Haka are imbued with deep meaning, often reflecting themes of courage, defiance, and respect for one's ancestors.

The All Blacks' association with the Haka began in the late 19th century. The first known performance by a New Zealand rugby team was in 1888 by the New Zealand Native football team, who performed the Haka during their tour of Britain. The tradition was further solidified in 1905 when the All Blacks embarked on their historic tour of the British Isles. Before their matches, they performed a Haka, captivating audiences and intimidating their opponents. This early adoption of the Haka set the stage for it to become an enduring tradition.

The words of the Haka performed by the All Blacks are often those of "Ka Mate," a Haka composed by the Māori chief Te Rauparaha in the early 19th century. "Ka Mate" tells the story of Te Rauparaha's escape from enemies and his gratitude to the gods for his survival. The chant begins with the words "Ka mate! Ka mate!" meaning "It is death! It is death!" and concludes with "Ka ora! Ka ora!" meaning "It is life! It is life!" The dramatic shift from despair to triumph mirrors the mindset required in rugby, where players must face their fears and emerge victorious.

The setting of the Haka is the rugby field, moments before the start of the match. The players, clad in their iconic black jerseys, assemble in formation, their faces set in expressions of fierce determination. The captain leads the Haka, initiating the chant with powerful words that echo across the stadium. The team responds in unison, their movements synchronised, creating a visual and auditory spectacle that sends shivers down the spines of spectators and opponents alike. The Haka serves as a psychological tool, instilling confidence in the All Blacks and striking fear into the hearts of their adversaries.

Over the years, the Haka has evolved, with the All Blacks introducing new versions to reflect different themes and messages. In 2005, to commemorate the centenary of the "Originals" tour, the All Blacks introduced "Kapa o Pango," a new Haka specifically created for the team. The words of "Kapa o Pango" celebrate the All Blacks' heritage and their connection to the land of New Zealand. The final line, "Ka tu te ihiihi," translates to "This defines us as the All Blacks." The introduction of "Kapa o Pango" demonstrated the team's commitment to honouring their roots while also forging their own unique identity.

The Haka has not been without controversy. Some opponents and commentators have questioned its place in modern rugby, arguing that it gives the All Blacks an unfair psychological advantage. Others have criticised certain elements of the Haka, such as the throat-slitting gesture in "Kapa o Pango," viewing them as overly aggressive. In response to these criticisms, the All Blacks have defended the Haka as a vital expression of their culture and identity, emphasising its significance beyond mere intimidation.

The Haka is more than a pre-match ritual; it is a unifying force for the All Blacks, binding the players together as they prepare for the physical and mental challenges of the game. It fosters a sense of camaraderie and shared purpose, reminding each player of the honour and responsibility of representing New Zealand. The Haka also serves as a tribute to the Māori culture, showcasing its beauty and power on the global stage. The respect and reverence with which the All Blacks perform the Haka underscore their deep connection to their heritage.

The impact of the Haka extends beyond the rugby field. It has become a symbol of New Zealand's national identity, embodying the spirit and resilience of the country's people. The Haka is performed at various national and international events, from welcoming dignitaries to celebrating achievements. It has also been adopted by other New Zealand sports teams, further cementing its role as a national emblem.

The All Blacks' dominance in rugby is closely intertwined with their performance of the Haka. The psychological impact of the Haka on their opponents cannot be overstated. It sets the tone for the match, establishing the All Blacks' presence and intent. The ritual has been credited with giving the team a mental edge, instilling a sense of invincibility that has translated into success on the field. The All Blacks have consistently been one of the top-ranked teams in the world, and their association with the Haka has played a significant role in their enduring legacy.

The Haka's influence is evident in some of the most memorable moments in rugby history. During the 1987 Rugby World Cup, held in New Zealand, the All Blacks performed the Haka with a renewed sense of purpose and pride, ultimately winning the tournament and becoming the first ever World Cup champions. The sight of the All Blacks performing the Haka before the final match against France remains an iconic image, symbolising their determination and unity.

Another memorable moment came during the 2011 Rugby World Cup, also held in New Zealand. The All Blacks faced France in the final, and the performance of the Haka before the match was particularly intense. The All Blacks went on to win the World Cup, ending a 24-year drought and solidifying their status as the best team in the world. The Haka, performed with passion and precision, was seen as a crucial factor in their victory.

The Haka has also been a source of inspiration for players and fans alike. It represents the values of respect, honour, and courage, qualities that resonate with athletes and supporters around the world. The All Blacks' commitment to the Haka is a testament to their dedication to preserving their cultural heritage and promoting the values it embodies.

The Haka has faced challenges and scrutiny over the years, but its significance remains undiminished. The All Blacks continue to perform the Haka with pride and respect, honouring their roots while embracing the evolution of the tradition. The ritual serves as a reminder of the power of culture and tradition to unite and inspire, transcending the boundaries of sport to become a symbol of national pride and identity.

The New Zealand All Blacks' Haka is a powerful and enduring tradition that has become an integral part of their identity. It is a testament to the team's connection to their Māori heritage and their commitment to honouring and preserving this important cultural practice. The Haka's influence extends beyond the rugby field, embodying the spirit and resilience of the New Zealand people. The All Blacks' performance of the Haka is a captivating spectacle that continues to inspire and captivate audiences around the world, symbolising the values of respect, honour, and courage.

Manchester United's 1999 Treble

Manchester United's 1999 Treble is one of the most remarkable achievements in football history, a season that saw the club win the Premier League, FA Cup, and UEFA Champions League. This unprecedented success was the result of a combination of talent, determination, and strategic brilliance, culminating in a series of unforgettable matches and moments.

The journey began under the leadership of Sir Alex Ferguson, a manager renowned for his tactical acumen and ability to inspire his players. Ferguson had been at the helm of Manchester United since 1986, steadily building a squad capable of competing at the highest levels. The team that entered the 1998-1999 season was a blend of experienced veterans and youthful exuberance, featuring players like Ryan Giggs, David Beckham, Roy Keane, and Peter Schmeichel, alongside emerging talents such as Paul Scholes and the Neville brothers.

The Premier League campaign was fiercely competitive, with United facing strong challenges from Arsenal and Chelsea. The season was characterised by a series of dramatic matches, where United's resilience and attacking prowess often saw them come from behind to secure crucial points. One such match was against Arsenal at Old Trafford, where a stunning last-minute goal from Giggs ensured a vital victory. The season also witnessed Beckham's exceptional ability to deliver precise crosses and free-kicks, which played a crucial role in many of United's victories.

Roy Keane's leadership in midfield was instrumental throughout the season. His tenacity and ability to break up opposition play provided a solid foundation for United's attacking talents. Scholes, with his vision and goal-scoring ability, became a pivotal figure, while the defensive solidity provided by Jaap Stam and the Neville brothers ensured United remained difficult to beat. Schmeichel's performances in goal were also critical, often making crucial saves that kept United in contention during tight matches.

The FA Cup run added another layer of excitement and tension to the season. The semi-final against Arsenal, played at Villa Park, was a particularly memorable encounter. With the match tied at 1-1, United were reduced to ten men after Keane was sent off. In extra time, Giggs scored one of the most iconic goals in FA Cup history, weaving his way through the Arsenal defence to secure a place in the final. This moment epitomised the spirit and determination of the team.

In the final against Newcastle United, United displayed their attacking flair and composure, winning 2-0 with goals from Teddy Sheringham and Paul Scholes. This victory secured the second part of the Treble and set the stage for the most challenging and dramatic part of their journey – the UEFA Champions League.

The Champions League campaign was a rollercoaster of emotions, filled with memorable matches and dramatic moments. United were drawn into a tough group alongside Bayern Munich, Barcelona, and Brøndby. The group stage featured thrilling encounters, including a high-scoring draw against Barcelona at the Camp Nou, where United's attacking trio of Dwight Yorke, Andy Cole, and Beckham showcased their potency.

The knockout stages brought further challenges, with United facing Inter Milan in the quarter-finals. A solid 2-0 victory at Old Trafford, thanks to goals from Yorke, set up a tense second leg in Milan. Despite intense pressure from Inter, United held on to secure their place in the semi-finals. The semi-final clash against Juventus was another test of United's resilience and character. After drawing 1-1 at Old Trafford, United faced a daunting task in the return leg in Turin. Juventus took an early 2-0 lead, but United mounted a stunning comeback with goals from Keane, Yorke, and Cole, securing a 3-2 victory and a place in the final.

The Champions League final, held at the Camp Nou in Barcelona, was a fitting climax to an extraordinary season. United faced Bayern Munich, a team they had already encountered in the group stage. The match began disastrously for United, with Bayern taking an early lead through Mario Basler's free-kick. Despite creating several chances, United struggled to find an equaliser, and as the clock ticked down, it seemed their hopes of a Treble were slipping away.

Ferguson made crucial substitutions, bringing on Sheringham and Ole Gunnar Solskjær in a desperate bid to turn the tide. As the match entered stoppage time, United won a corner. Beckham delivered the ball into the box, and after a scramble, it fell to Sheringham, who instinctively turned it into the net, levelling the score. The drama was far from over, as moments later, another corner led to Solskjær's dramatic winner, poking the ball past the Bayern goalkeeper and completing one of the most incredible comebacks in football history.

The scenes of jubilation among the United players and fans were unforgettable. Ferguson's faith in his squad and his tactical genius had paid off in the most spectacular fashion. The victory secured the Treble, an achievement that no other English club had accomplished before. The players' celebrations on the pitch reflected the culmination of a season of hard work, resilience, and sheer determination.

The triumph in 1999 was not just about the trophies; it was a testament to the spirit and unity of the team. Ferguson's management was crucial in fostering a winning mentality and a sense of belief that saw the team overcome numerous obstacles. The blend of experienced players and young talents created a perfect balance, allowing United to compete on multiple fronts and succeed.

Beckham's precision from set-pieces, Giggs' dribbling ability, Keane's leadership, and Schmeichel's shot-stopping prowess were all key components of United's success. The striking partnership of Yorke and Cole was particularly potent, with their understanding and goal-scoring ability causing problems for defences throughout the season. The contributions of Sheringham and Solskjær, often from the bench, highlighted the depth and quality of the squad.

The 1999 Treble season also had a profound impact on the club's legacy and the careers of the players involved. It cemented Ferguson's status as one of the greatest managers in football history and laid the foundation for future successes. The players became legends, their names etched into the annals of the club's history. The achievements of that season continue to be celebrated by United fans, a reminder of a period when the team reached the pinnacle of European football.

The success also had a wider impact on English football, inspiring other clubs to strive for similar heights. It demonstrated the importance of squad depth, tactical flexibility, and mental toughness in achieving sustained success across multiple competitions. The Treble-winning season remains a benchmark for excellence and a source of pride for Manchester United and its supporters.

The legacy of the 1999 Treble endures, not just in the trophies won, but in the memories of the dramatic moments, the incredible comebacks, and the unbreakable spirit of the team. It was a season that encapsulated the essence of football – the highs and lows, the triumphs and challenges, and the joy of achieving the seemingly impossible. The story of Manchester United's 1999 Treble is a testament to the power of belief, the strength of teamwork, and the magic of the beautiful game.

The Boston Red Sox's 2004 World Series Win

The Boston Red Sox's 2004 World Series win is one of the most iconic moments in baseball history, marked by a dramatic and triumphant journey that broke an 86-year championship drought. This victory was the culmination of decades of heartbreak, near-misses, and a storied rivalry with the New York Yankees. The 2004 season was a testament to resilience, determination, and the power of belief.

The story of the 2004 Boston Red Sox is intertwined with the legendary "Curse of the Bambino," a superstition that began when the Red Sox sold Babe Ruth to the Yankees in 1919. This curse was blamed for the Red Sox's numerous failed attempts to win the World Series over the ensuing decades. As the years passed, the curse became a part of Boston lore, with each near-miss and heartbreaking loss adding to the mythology.

Entering the 2004 season, the Red Sox had assembled a formidable team under the leadership of General Manager Theo Epstein and Manager Terry Francona. Epstein, known for his analytical approach, had crafted a roster blending power, pitching, and depth. Key players included Manny Ramirez, David Ortiz, Johnny Damon, and Curt Schilling, each of whom would play crucial roles in the season's narrative.

Fenway Park, the hallowed home of the Red Sox, provided the setting for many memorable moments throughout the season. The stadium, with its iconic Green Monster and passionate fans, became a fortress where the team drew inspiration and energy. The atmosphere at Fenway was electric, as the fans, ever hopeful, filled the stands with their unwavering support.

The Red Sox started the season strong, showcasing their potent offense and solid pitching staff. Ramirez and Ortiz formed a formidable duo, known for their clutch hitting and ability to change the course of a game with a single swing. Schilling, acquired from the Arizona Diamondbacks, brought veteran leadership and a fierce competitive spirit to the pitching rotation. Alongside Pedro Martinez, Derek Lowe, and Tim Wakefield, Schilling helped anchor a staff capable of shutting down even the most potent lineups.

As the season progressed, the Red Sox faced their fair share of challenges. Injuries, slumps, and stiff competition tested the team's mettle. However, they persevered, driven by a collective belief that this could be the year to end the curse. The regular season saw the Red Sox secure a playoff berth, finishing second in the American League East behind the Yankees.

The postseason began with the American League Division Series (ALDS) against the Anaheim Angels. The Red Sox quickly demonstrated their dominance, sweeping the Angels in three games. Ortiz and Ramirez continued their clutch hitting, while Schilling and Martinez delivered strong performances on the mound. This sweep set the stage for an epic confrontation with their arch-rivals, the New York Yankees, in the American League Championship Series (ALCS).

The ALCS was a rematch of the previous year's series, which had ended in heartbreak for the Red Sox. The Yankees took a commanding 3-0 lead in the series, pushing the Red Sox to the brink of elimination. No team in Major League Baseball history had ever come back from a 3-0 deficit to win a seven-game series. The situation seemed dire, but the Red Sox refused to give up.

Game 4 at Fenway Park was a turning point. The game went into extra innings, and in the 12th inning, David Ortiz hit a walk-off two-run homer to give the Red Sox a 6-4 victory, staving off elimination. Ortiz's heroics earned him the nickname "Big Papi" and solidified his status as a Boston legend. The win injected new life into the team and the fanbase.

Game 5 was another marathon affair, lasting 14 innings. Once again, Ortiz delivered in the clutch, hitting a walk-off single to win the game 5-4. The Red Sox had clawed their way back, winning two consecutive extra-inning games and shifting the momentum of the series. The resilient performances of the bullpen, including key contributions from Keith Foulke and Tim Wakefield, were instrumental in these victories.

The series returned to Yankee Stadium for Game 6, where Curt Schilling delivered one of the most iconic performances in baseball history. Pitching with a torn tendon in his ankle, Schilling's sock was visibly stained with blood. Despite the pain, he pitched seven innings, allowing just one run and leading the Red Sox to a 4-2 victory. Schilling's gritty performance became known as the "Bloody Sock Game," symbolising the team's determination and toughness.

Game 7 was a decisive showdown. The Red Sox dominated from the start, with Johnny Damon hitting two home runs, including a grand slam, to propel the team to a 10-3 victory. The Red Sox had completed the greatest comeback in baseball history, winning the series 4-3 and earning a trip to the World Series. The victory over the Yankees was particularly sweet, as it ended years of torment at the hands of their rivals and exorcised some of the ghosts of the past.

The World Series saw the Red Sox face the St. Louis Cardinals, a team with a rich history and a formidable lineup. The Red Sox entered the series with confidence and momentum, determined to end the curse once and for all. Game 1 at Fenway Park set the tone, with the Red Sox winning a high-scoring affair 11-9. Ramirez and Ortiz continued to lead the offense, while the pitching staff held strong.

Game 2 saw Curt Schilling take the mound once again, pitching through pain and delivering a gutsy performance. The Red Sox won 6-2, taking a 2-0 series lead. The series then shifted to Busch Stadium in St. Louis, where the Red Sox maintained their dominance. Game 3 featured a masterful performance by Pedro Martinez, who pitched seven scoreless innings to lead the Red Sox to a 4-1 victory.

With a 3-0 series lead, the Red Sox were on the cusp of history. Game 4 was a tightly contested affair, with Derek Lowe delivering a strong performance on the mound. The Red Sox took an early lead, and the bullpen held firm. In the ninth inning, with the Red Sox leading 3-0, Keith Foulke induced a ground ball from Edgar Renteria, which he fielded cleanly and tossed to first baseman Doug Mientkiewicz for the final out.

The moment was surreal. The Boston Red Sox had won the World Series, ending an 86-year championship drought. The players erupted in celebration, and the fans rejoiced. Fenway Park and the streets of Boston were filled with jubilant supporters, many of whom had waited their entire lives for this moment. The victory was a culmination of years of perseverance, resilience, and unwavering belief.

The triumph of the 2004 Boston Red Sox was a team effort, with contributions from every player on the roster. Manny Ramirez, named World Series MVP, showcased his incredible hitting ability throughout the postseason. David Ortiz's clutch performances earned him legendary status in Boston. Curt Schilling's heroics, Pedro Martinez's brilliance, and the bullpen's steadfastness were all crucial to the team's success.

The 2004 World Series win also marked a turning point for the Red Sox franchise. It lifted the burden of the curse and paved the way for future successes. The Red Sox would go on to win additional championships in 2007, 2013, and 2018, establishing themselves as one of the premier franchises in Major League Baseball.

The legacy of the 2004 Boston Red Sox is one of resilience, belief, and triumph. It is a story of overcoming adversity, of never giving up, and of achieving the seemingly impossible. The journey to the World Series title was filled with dramatic moments, heroic performances, and unforgettable memories. The victory not only brought joy to Red Sox fans but also left an indelible mark on the history of baseball.

Leicester City's Premier League Title (2015-2016)

The Rumble in the Jungle (1974)

The Rumble in the Jungle, held on October 30, 1974, in Kinshasa, Zaire, remains one of the most iconic boxing matches in history. This epic confrontation between Muhammad Ali and George Foreman was more than just a fight; it was a cultural and political event that captivated the world. Muhammad Ali, born Cassius Clay, was already a legendary figure by the time he faced Foreman. Ali's charisma, quick wit, and unmatched boxing skills had made him a global icon. He won the heavyweight title in 1964 by defeating Sonny Liston, and his conversion to Islam and subsequent name change to Muhammad Ali further solidified his status as a controversial and influential figure.

George Foreman, in contrast, was a younger and less flamboyant character but equally formidable in the ring. Born in Marshall, Texas, Foreman was known for his incredible punching power. He had won the gold medal at the 1968 Olympics and quickly made a name for himself in professional boxing. Foreman's path to the heavyweight title was marked by devastating knockouts, and in 1973, he demolished Joe Frazier to win the title, sending shockwaves through the boxing world. Foreman's dominance was such that many believed he was unbeatable.

The idea of staging the fight in Zaire was the brainchild of promoter Don King. King, known for his flamboyant personality and promotional prowess, saw an opportunity to make history by taking the fight out of the traditional venues and into Africa. President Mobutu Sese Seko of Zaire saw the fight as a chance to showcase his country on the global stage and agreed to finance the event. The setting in Kinshasa, with its rich cultural heritage and vibrant atmosphere, provided a unique backdrop for the showdown.

Leading up to the fight, the contrast between Ali and Foreman was stark. Ali, despite his previous successes, was seen by many as the underdog. His unorthodox style, characterised by his speed, agility, and psychological tactics, had previously baffled opponents, but he was now facing a younger, stronger, and seemingly invincible champion. Foreman, with his stoic demeanour and devastating power, was favoured to retain his title. The hype surrounding the fight was immense, with media from around the world descending on Kinshasa to cover the event.

Ali's preparation for the fight was meticulous. He understood that Foreman's power was his greatest asset and that a head-on confrontation could be disastrous. Ali's trainer, Angelo Dundee, crafted a strategy that would later be known as the "rope-a-dope." This involved Ali leaning back against the ropes, allowing Foreman to unleash his powerful punches while Ali absorbed the blows with his arms and gloves. The idea was to tire Foreman out, exploiting his tendency to exhaust himself with aggressive attacks.

The atmosphere in Kinshasa was electric in the days leading up to the fight. Ali's charisma and connection with the local people endeared him to the crowd. He embraced the culture, frequently interacting with the public and participating in local events. The chants of "Ali, boma ye!" which means "Ali, kill him!" echoed through the streets, reflecting the local support for Ali. Foreman, on the other hand, maintained a more reserved presence, focusing on his training and preparation.

When fight night arrived, the 20th of May Stadium was filled to capacity, with tens of thousands of spectators eagerly anticipating the clash. The heat and humidity of the African night added to the intensity of the occasion. As the fighters entered the ring, the contrast in their demeanours was apparent. Ali exuded confidence, dancing and taunting Foreman, while Foreman remained stoic and focused, intent on retaining his title.

From the opening bell, the fight was a tactical battle. Foreman came out aggressively, throwing powerful punches that forced Ali to retreat. Ali employed the rope-a-dope strategy, leaning against the ropes and allowing Foreman to expend energy with each punch. Foreman's blows were powerful, but Ali's defensive skills and ability to absorb punishment were remarkable. As the rounds progressed, it became clear that Ali's strategy was working. Foreman's punches began to lose their power, and his movements grew slower and more laboured.

By the middle rounds, Ali began to take advantage of Foreman's fatigue. He started to throw quick jabs and combinations, scoring points and further frustrating Foreman. Ali's taunting and psychological tactics added to Foreman's frustration, causing him to make mistakes and expend even more energy. The crowd, already firmly behind Ali, grew louder with each successful punch.

In the eighth round, the culmination of Ali's strategy became evident. Foreman, exhausted and struggling to defend himself, left an opening. Ali seized the moment, delivering a series of precise and powerful punches. A right-hand lead, followed by a left hook and another right hand, sent Foreman crashing to the canvas. The crowd erupted in celebration as the referee counted to ten, signalling the end of the fight. Ali had done the impossible; he had defeated the seemingly invincible George Foreman and reclaimed the heavyweight title.

The victory was not just a triumph for Ali, but for the millions of fans who had supported him through his career. It was a vindication of his resilience, his tactical brilliance, and his unwavering belief in himself. Ali's performance in Kinshasa solidified his status as one of the greatest boxers of all time and a global icon. The fight itself became a symbol of the power of strategy, intelligence, and psychological warfare in sports.

In the aftermath of the fight, Ali's status as a cultural and political icon grew even stronger. He continued to use his platform to speak out on issues of social justice, civil rights, and global peace. Foreman, despite his defeat, showed great sportsmanship and humility. He took time away from boxing but eventually returned, reinventing himself and becoming a beloved figure in his own right.

The Rumble in the Jungle had a profound impact on the sport of boxing and on popular culture. It demonstrated the importance of strategy and intelligence in a sport often dominated by brute strength. Ali's rope-a-dope strategy became legendary, studied by fighters and trainers for years to come. The fight also highlighted the global appeal of boxing, bringing the sport to new audiences and inspiring a generation of fighters.

The fight in Kinshasa remains a defining moment in the history of sports. It was a night when two of the greatest heavyweights of all time faced off in a battle of wills, skills, and endurance. Ali's victory was a triumph of the human spirit, a testament to his ability to overcome adversity and defy the odds. The Rumble in the Jungle will forever be remembered as one of the most extraordinary events in the history of boxing, a night when Muhammad Ali truly proved he was "The Greatest."

The 2021 Abu Dhabi Grand Prix

The 2021 Abu Dhabi Grand Prix, held at the Yas Marina Circuit on December 12th, was one of the most dramatic and controversial races in Formula 1 history. The season-long battle between Lewis Hamilton and Max Verstappen for the World Championship came to a head in this final race, captivating fans around the globe. Yas Marina Circuit, with its stunning backdrop of the Arabian Gulf and futuristic architecture, provided the perfect setting for the climax of a fiercely contested season.

Lewis Hamilton, the seven-time World Champion, was chasing a record-breaking eighth title. Driving for Mercedes, Hamilton had demonstrated remarkable consistency and skill throughout the season. His experience and tactical acumen were on full display as he navigated through a season filled with ups and downs. Mercedes, led by team principal Toto Wolff, had once again provided Hamilton with a car capable of competing at the highest level. The W12 was a powerful machine, known for its speed and reliability.

Max Verstappen, the young and fearless driver for Red Bull Racing, had emerged as Hamilton's main rival. Verstappen, known for his aggressive driving style and relentless pursuit of victory, was determined to win his first World Championship. Red Bull, under the leadership of team principal Christian Horner, had produced the RB16B, a car that matched Mercedes in performance. Adrian Newey, Red Bull's chief technical officer, played a crucial role in designing a car that could challenge Mercedes' dominance.

The 2021 season was marked by intense rivalry and numerous clashes between Hamilton and Verstappen. The British Grand Prix at

Silverstone saw a major incident where Hamilton and Verstappen collided, resulting in Verstappen crashing out of the race. This incident ignited further tensions between the two drivers and their respective teams. The Italian Grand Prix at Monza witnessed another dramatic collision, with both drivers being forced to retire from the race. These incidents added fuel to an already heated championship battle, setting the stage for a thrilling finale in Abu Dhabi.

As the teams arrived in Abu Dhabi, the tension was palpable. Both Hamilton and Verstappen were level on points, a scenario not seen since 1974. The Yas Marina Circuit, known for its unique layout and twilight race conditions, posed a significant challenge. The circuit's long straights and tight corners required a perfect balance of speed and precision. The backdrop of the sun setting over the marina added to the sense of occasion, creating a visually stunning and atmospheric setting for the race.

Qualifying was fiercely contested, with Verstappen securing pole position in a dramatic session. His lap, aided by a tow from teammate Sergio Perez, put him ahead of Hamilton, who qualified second. The front row lockout by Red Bull added to the anticipation, with many expecting a fierce battle from the very start. The atmosphere in the paddock was electric, with teams, drivers, and fans eagerly awaiting the start of the race.

As the lights went out, Hamilton made a lightning start, overtaking Verstappen into the first corner. The race quickly settled into a rhythm, with Hamilton leading and Verstappen in close pursuit. The opening laps were tense, with both drivers pushing their cars to the limit. Verstappen's aggressive driving style was on full display, as he tried to find a way past Hamilton. The two drivers were in a league of their own, pulling away from the rest of the field.

Midway through the race, Red Bull made a strategic call, pitting Verstappen for fresh tyres. Mercedes responded by pitting Hamilton, maintaining his lead. The strategic battle between the two teams added another layer of intrigue to the race. Verstappen's fresh tyres gave him a performance advantage, but Hamilton's experience and racecraft allowed him to maintain his lead.

The race took a dramatic turn on lap 53 when Nicholas Latifi crashed, bringing out the safety car. This incident set the stage for one of the most controversial moments in Formula 1 history. Red Bull pitted Verstappen for a fresh set of soft tyres, while Mercedes kept Hamilton out on his older hard tyres. The decision to pit Verstappen was a gamble, but one that paid off in spectacular fashion.

As the safety car period ended, race director Michael Masi made the decision to allow the lapped cars between Hamilton and Verstappen to un-lap themselves. This decision, made in the heat of the moment, sparked controversy and debate. It meant that Verstappen was directly behind Hamilton on the restart, with fresher and faster tyres. The stage was set for a final lap showdown.

At the restart, Verstappen made his move, diving down the inside of Hamilton into turn five. The two cars went wheel-to-wheel, with Verstappen emerging ahead. Hamilton fought back, but Verstappen's grip advantage was decisive. As they rounded the final corners, Verstappen held his lead, crossing the line to win the race and secure his first World Championship.

The scenes of celebration from the Red Bull team contrasted sharply with the disappointment and disbelief in the Mercedes garage. Verstappen's victory was a moment of triumph for Red Bull and a testament to his skill and determination. For Hamilton, it was a bitter pill to swallow, having come so close to a historic eighth title. The controversy surrounding the safety car decision and the final lap added to the drama, ensuring that the 2021 Abu Dhabi Grand Prix would be remembered for years to come.

The aftermath of the race saw heated discussions and debates within the Formula 1 community. Mercedes lodged protests against the race results, arguing that the rules regarding the safety car procedure had not been followed correctly. These protests were dismissed by the FIA, but the controversy continued to simmer. The 2021 season, with its intense rivalry and dramatic conclusion, had left an indelible mark on the sport.

In the days following the race, there was widespread speculation about the future of Lewis Hamilton. Many wondered if the disappointment of Abu Dhabi would lead him to consider retirement. Hamilton, however, remained composed and dignified, congratulating Verstappen on his victory. His sportsmanship in the face of adversity was widely praised, highlighting his status as a true champion.

Verstappen's title win marked the beginning of a new era in Formula 1. His aggressive driving style and fearless approach had won him many admirers, and his rivalry with Hamilton was expected to continue in the coming seasons. The 2021 Abu Dhabi Grand Prix, with its drama and controversy, had added a new chapter to the rich history of the sport.

The Yas Marina Circuit, with its state-of-the-art facilities and stunning backdrop, had provided the perfect setting for this historic race. The twilight conditions, with the sun setting over the marina, created a visually spectacular and atmospheric setting for the grand finale. The circuit, with its long straights and tight corners, had tested the drivers to the limit, providing a fitting stage for the championship decider.

The 2021 Abu Dhabi Grand Prix will be remembered as one of the most dramatic and controversial races in Formula 1 history. The intense rivalry between Hamilton and Verstappen, the strategic battles between Mercedes and Red Bull, and the dramatic final lap showdown had captivated fans around the world. The race was a testament to the skill, determination, and competitive spirit of the drivers and teams, highlighting the thrill and unpredictability of Formula 1.

Leicester City's Premier League Title (2015-2016)

Leicester City's 2015-2016 Premier League title win is one of the most extraordinary stories in football history. The journey to this triumph was marked by perseverance, resilience, and a perfect blend of talent and strategy. The club, often considered an underdog in English football, defied all odds to achieve a feat that stunned the world.

Leicester City, based in the East Midlands, had a long and varied history in English football. The club, founded in 1884, spent much of its existence outside the top flight. In 2008, Leicester faced the ignominy of relegation to League One, the third tier of English football. However, they quickly bounced back, earning promotion to the Championship the following year. The climb continued, and in 2014, Leicester City returned to the Premier League after a decade-long absence. The 2014-2015 season saw them narrowly avoid relegation, finishing 14th after a dramatic late-season surge under manager Nigel Pearson.

The summer of 2015 brought significant changes. Nigel Pearson was sacked, and Claudio Ranieri was appointed as the new manager. Ranieri, an experienced coach with a wealth of experience across Europe, was seen as an unusual choice by many. His previous stints included managing top clubs like Chelsea, Valencia, and Roma, but he had never won a major league title. Expectations for Leicester were modest, with most pundits predicting another struggle to avoid relegation.

Ranieri, however, brought a calm and pragmatic approach to the team. He retained much of the squad from the previous season but made a few astute signings. N'Golo Kanté, a relatively unknown midfielder from Caen, was brought in to add energy and tenacity to the midfield.

Christian Fuchs, a seasoned Austrian defender, joined on a free transfer, providing experience and stability to the back line. Japanese forward Shinji Okazaki was signed to bolster the attack. These additions, combined with the existing core of players, created a squad that was balanced, hard-working, and full of character.

The heart of the team was the partnership between Wes Morgan and Robert Huth in central defence. Morgan, the club captain, was a commanding presence, known for his leadership and physicality. Huth, a seasoned Premier League defender, complemented Morgan with his no-nonsense approach and aerial dominance. In goal, Kasper Schmeichel, son of legendary goalkeeper Peter Schmeichel, provided security and inspiration with his shot-stopping ability and vocal leadership.

The midfield was transformed by the arrival of Kanté. His tireless running, ball-winning skills, and ability to cover ground made him the engine of the team. Alongside him, Danny Drinkwater provided composure and vision, orchestrating play from deep positions. The wide areas were patrolled by Marc Albrighton and Riyad Mahrez. Albrighton's work rate and delivery from the flanks were crucial, while Mahrez's flair, dribbling, and creativity added a touch of magic to the side.

Up front, Jamie Vardy led the line with relentless pace and determination. Vardy's journey to the top was remarkable. Having played in non-league football until his mid-twenties, his rise to the Premier League was a testament to his hard work and perseverance. Vardy's speed and finishing made him a constant threat, and he thrived in Leicester's counter-attacking system.

Leicester's season began with an impressive run of form. They won their opening match against Sunderland 4-2, showcasing their attacking intent and resilience. This early success was not seen as a sign of things to come, but as the weeks passed, Leicester continued to defy expectations. They played with a fearless attitude, pressing high, breaking quickly, and showing incredible work rate.

One of the defining features of Leicester's campaign was their ability to win games by narrow margins. They often scored first and defended resolutely to protect their lead. Ranieri's tactical acumen was evident in the way he set up his team. He utilised a 4-4-2 formation, with Vardy and Okazaki pressing from the front, Kanté and Drinkwater providing solidity in the middle, and Mahrez given the freedom to create.

By the end of November, Leicester were top of the league, a position they had not occupied since 2000. Many still doubted their ability to maintain their form, expecting the traditional powerhouses like Manchester City, Arsenal, and Manchester United to overtake them. However, Leicester's consistency and belief grew stronger with each passing week.

The turning point of the season came in February when Leicester faced Manchester City at the Etihad Stadium. The match was seen as a test of their title credentials. Leicester produced a stunning performance, winning 3-1 with goals from Huth and Mahrez. This victory sent shockwaves through the league and firmly established Leicester as genuine title contenders.

Another crucial moment was Vardy's record-breaking goal-scoring run. He scored in 11 consecutive Premier League matches, breaking the record previously held by Ruud van Nistelrooy. Vardy's form was instrumental in Leicester's success, and his goalscoring exploits captured the imagination of football fans around the world.

As the season progressed, Leicester's lead at the top of the table grew. They displayed remarkable consistency, losing only three matches all season. Their defence, marshalled by Morgan and Huth, was resolute, and Schmeichel's performances in goal were outstanding. Kanté's influence in midfield was undeniable, and Mahrez's creativity and flair provided the spark in attack. The camaraderie and spirit within the squad were palpable, with every player contributing to the collective effort.

The final weeks of the season were filled with anticipation and excitement. Leicester's closest challengers, Tottenham Hotspur, were also in impressive form, but Leicester's consistency proved too much. On May 2, 2016, Leicester were crowned Premier League champions after Tottenham could only draw against Chelsea. The celebrations that followed were euphoric. The players, staff, and fans reveled in the achievement, knowing they had witnessed something truly special.

Leicester's title win was not just a sporting triumph; it was a story of hope, resilience, and the power of belief. It showed that with the right blend of talent, hard work, and unity, even the most improbable dreams could be realised. The players became legends, with Vardy, Mahrez, Kanté, and others etching their names into football history.

The impact of Leicester's triumph was felt far beyond the club. It inspired football fans around the world, demonstrating that anything is possible in the beautiful game. The financial disparity between Leicester and the traditional giants of English football made their achievement even more remarkable. It was a victory for the underdog, a reminder that football is not just about money and star power, but about teamwork, passion, and heart.

In the aftermath of their title win, Leicester faced new challenges. Kanté left for Chelsea, but the core of the squad remained. They embarked on a Champions League campaign, reaching the quarter-finals and continuing to defy expectations. The spirit and resilience that had defined their title-winning season remained intact, and they continued to compete at a high level.

Claudio Ranieri, the mastermind behind the triumph, received widespread acclaim for his role. His calm and pragmatic approach, combined with his ability to get the best out of his players, were key factors in Leicester's success. Ranieri's humility and warmth endeared him to fans and players alike, and he became a beloved figure in Leicester's history.

Leicester's 2015-2016 Premier League title win will forever be remembered as one of the greatest achievements in sports history. It was a season that captured the imagination of football fans everywhere, a fairy tale that showed the magic of the sport. The characters, the settings, and the journey all combined to create a story that will be told for generations to come. Leicester City's triumph was a victory for football, a celebration of the unpredictable and the extraordinary, and a testament to the enduring power of hope and belief.

The 1994 Olympics: Tonya Harding and Nancy Kerrigan

The 1994 Lillehammer Olympics Women's Figure Skating event captivated the world not only for the grace and skill displayed on the ice but also for the dramatic saga that unfolded off the rink. At the center of this tumultuous tale were two American figure skaters: Tonya Harding and Nancy Kerrigan. Their rivalry, fueled by ambition, jealousy, and controversy, reached its climax during the lead-up to the Winter Games in Norway.

Tonya Harding emerged from a turbulent upbringing to become one of America's top figure skaters. Raised in Portland, Oregon, Harding faced numerous challenges from an early age. Her mother, LaVona Golden, was notoriously tough on her daughter, pushing her relentlessly to excel in figure skating. Despite the financial struggles her family faced, Harding's talent on the ice was undeniable. With her powerful jumps and aggressive style, she quickly rose through the ranks of the figure skating world.

In contrast, Nancy Kerrigan hailed from a more privileged background. Born and raised in Stoneham, Massachusetts, Kerrigan received extensive support from her family in pursuing her skating dreams. Blessed with natural elegance and grace, she captured the hearts of fans with her fluid movements and impeccable technique. Kerrigan's rise to prominence was marked by success in national and international competitions, earning her a reputation as one of America's brightest skating stars.

The stage was set for a showdown between Harding and Kerrigan at the 1994 Winter Olympics in Lillehammer, Norway. Both skaters were vying for the coveted gold medal, but tensions simmered beneath the surface. In the months leading up to the Games, rumors swirled of discord between Harding and Kerrigan, fueled by their intense rivalry and competitive spirit.

The rivalry between Harding and Kerrigan came to a head on January 6, 1994, when Kerrigan was attacked during a practice session at the U.S. Figure Skating Championships in Detroit. As Kerrigan stepped off the ice, a man later identified as Shane Stant struck her with a metal baton, aiming for her right knee. The assault left Kerrigan writhing in pain, clutching her injured leg and crying out for help.

The attack sent shockwaves through the figure skating world and captured the attention of the media worldwide. As Kerrigan underwent medical treatment for her injured knee, speculation swirled about the motive behind the assault. Was it a random act of violence, or was there something more sinister at play?

Authorities soon uncovered a web of conspiracy surrounding the attack, implicating individuals connected to Harding's inner circle. Harding's ex-husband, Jeff Gillooly, and her bodyguard, Shawn Eckardt, were arrested and charged with planning and carrying out the assault on Kerrigan. Harding herself was implicated in the plot, accused of conspiring to hinder the prosecution of those involved.

As the investigation unfolded, Harding maintained her innocence, insisting that she had no prior knowledge of the attack on Kerrigan. However, evidence surfaced suggesting otherwise, including testimony from Gillooly and Eckardt implicating Harding in the conspiracy. The scandal tarnished Harding's reputation and cast a shadow over her Olympic aspirations.

Despite the controversy surrounding her, Harding pressed on with her preparations for the Winter Olympics. In a dramatic turn of events, both Harding and Kerrigan were selected to represent the United States at the Games, setting the stage for a highly anticipated showdown on the ice.

The women's figure skating event at the 1994 Lillehammer Olympics was a spectacle unlike any other, with the eyes of the world watching as Harding and Kerrigan took to the ice. Amidst the glare of the spotlight, Kerrigan delivered a flawless performance, showcasing her grace and artistry with each elegant movement.

Harding, meanwhile, struggled to maintain her composure under the weight of scrutiny and controversy. Despite her undeniable talent, Harding's nerves got the better of her, leading to a series of missteps and mistakes during her performance. As the final scores were tallied, Kerrigan emerged victorious, claiming the silver medal while Harding finished in eighth place.

The aftermath of the 1994 Lillehammer Olympics marked the end of an era for both Harding and Kerrigan. Kerrigan went on to enjoy continued success in the world of figure skating, earning accolades and admiration for her resilience and grace under pressure. Harding, on the other hand, saw her career unravel in the wake of the scandal, facing backlash and ostracism from the skating community.

The saga of Tonya Harding and Nancy Kerrigan remains one of the most memorable chapters in the history of figure skating. Their rivalry, marked by triumph and tragedy, serves as a cautionary tale of the perils of fame, ambition, and the pursuit of glory at any cost. As the world looks back on the events of 1994, the legacy of Harding and Kerrigan endures as a reminder of the highs and lows of athletic competition.

Ford and Ferrari at the 24 Hours of Le Mans

In the exhilarating world of motorsport, few narratives resonate as deeply as the historic clash between Ford and Ferrari at the 24 Hours of Le Mans. This titanic showdown, set against the vibrant backdrop of the swinging sixties, remains etched in the annals of racing lore as a testament to the unyielding pursuit of victory and the fierce rivalry between two automotive titans.

The genesis of this epic rivalry can be traced back to the early 1960s when Henry Ford II, the ambitious scion of the Ford Motor Company, set his sights on conquering the world of endurance racing. Inspired by the dominance of European manufacturers like Ferrari at prestigious events such as the 24 Hours of Le Mans, Ford resolved to establish his company as a formidable force in motorsport, thus setting the stage for an audacious confrontation.

At the helm of Ford's ambitious venture was Carroll Shelby, a charismatic figure whose exploits as a racing driver and automotive designer had earned him a reputation as a maverick and a visionary. Shelby, tasked with spearheading Ford's racing program, relished the opportunity to take on Ferrari, viewing the Italian marque with a mixture of admiration and disdain.

Shelby, known for his flamboyant personality and his penchant for stirring up controversy, wasted no time in provoking Ferrari at every turn. With characteristic bravado, Shelby taunted Ferrari, publicly challenging them to a head-to-head showdown at Le Mans and daring them to take on Ford's formidable racing team.

Meanwhile, Ken Miles, a British racing driver and mechanical virtuoso, emerged as a pivotal figure in Ford's quest for victory. Renowned for his meticulous attention to detail and his uncanny ability to extract maximum performance from a machine, Miles played an indispensable role in the development and testing of the Ford GT40, pushing the car to its limits in pursuit of speed and reliability.

As Ford poured millions of dollars into the development of their racing program, Ferrari remained steadfast in their belief in the superiority of their machines. However, cracks began to appear in Ferrari's armor as Ford's relentless pursuit of victory began to yield results. In 1964, Ford GT40 prototypes made their debut at Le Mans, but mechanical failures thwarted their efforts, leaving Ferrari to claim yet another victory.

Undeterred by their initial setback, Ford redoubled their efforts, refining the GT40 and addressing the technical issues that had plagued their first attempt. In 1965, Ford returned to Le Mans with a renewed sense of purpose, determined to dethrone Ferrari and claim victory on the hallowed tarmac of Circuit de la Sarthe.

The stage was set for a showdown of epic proportions as Ford and Ferrari locked horns once again at Le Mans in 1966. The Ford GT40, now equipped with more powerful engines and improved aerodynamics, faced off against Ferrari's formidable stable of racing machines, including the legendary 330 P3.

From the moment the green flag dropped, it was clear that this would be a battle for the ages. Ford and Ferrari traded blows throughout the race, each pushing their machines to the limit in pursuit of victory. As day turned to night and fatigue began to take its toll, the outcome hung in the balance.

In the final hours of the race, it was Ford who emerged triumphant, with three GT40s crossing the finish line in a historic 1-2-3 sweep. However, controversy marred Ford's victory as Ken Miles, who had played a pivotal role in securing the win, was denied the opportunity to claim victory himself.

Despite leading the race for much of the event, Miles was instructed by Ford executives to slow down in the final moments, allowing his teammate, Bruce McLaren, to take the checkered flag and secure the win. The decision was met with outrage from fans and competitors alike, who believed that Miles had been robbed of victory in a cruel twist of fate.

For Ferrari, defeat at Le Mans was a bitter pill to swallow, marking the end of their dominance on the endurance racing scene. Enzo Ferrari, ever the proud and stubborn patriarch, begrudgingly acknowledged Ford's achievement but vowed to return stronger and more determined than ever.

In the years that followed, Ford and Ferrari continued to clash on the racetrack, each pushing the boundaries of automotive engineering in pursuit of victory. Their rivalry became the stuff of legend, inspiring generations of motorsport enthusiasts and immortalizing the iconic battles fought at Le Mans in the annals of motorsport history.

As the sun set on the swinging sixties, the legacy of Ford vs. Ferrari at Le Mans endured as a testament to the indomitable spirit of competition and the unyielding pursuit of excellence. In the crucible of endurance racing, two automotive giants had clashed, and from the flames of their rivalry had emerged a new era of motorsport greatness.

Printed in Great Britain
by Amazon